Practical Techniques to Enhance Your Sketching Skills

Masona M. Martinez

COPYRIGHT © 2023 Masona M. Martinez

All rights reserved.

Begin to be now what you will be hereafter. - William James

I attribute my success to this - I never gave or took any excuse. - Florence Nightingale

I know not age, nor weariness nor defeat. - Rose Kennedy

Whatever you want in life, other people are going to want it too. Believe in yourself enough to accept the idea that you have an equal right to it. - Diane Sawyer

The advantages of taking up sketching as a hobby

Have you been searching for your next project to keep yourself busy, educated, and content? Maybe learning to draw has been on your bucket list, but you don't know where to begin, you're anxious to do it correctly, or you're not sure the rewards will be worthwhile. Well…

There are MANY Advantages to Drawing for a Better Life!

We'll examine eight of them.

an improved sense of self.

The majority of people put off creating art (even when they want to) because they believe they will never be good at it, but this couldn't be further from the truth! Research backs up the growth mindset, which holds that no one is born "good at" anything and that learning new skills takes time and patience. Every day of the journey has beauty and meaning.

ALL art has its own fabulousness, and once you realize that what you produce is wonderful—even if it differs from other people's work—you'll suddenly find new opportunities for self-love in other areas of your life where you've been lacking self-assurance.

The Strength of Having a Project in Boosting Mental Health.

Having a long-term project is one of the best things a person can do to feel happier. You can always make progress on a project while also learning from it. An illustration of this is the zest for life that comes from a multi-week exercise regimen or starting the journey of consuming more fruits and vegetables. Taking on the endeavor of learning to draw is another illustration!

The wonderful thing about making art exploration your ongoing project is that your search is never over. If you're feeling down or bored, pick up a pencil to lift your spirits because we can always improve our ability and style and remain in that liminal space of learning.

Relaxation with the "Flow" Meditation.

Being in a "state of flow" is a phenomenon that is incredibly calming and energizing when it comes to soothing the soul. You've probably already experienced flow, which occurs when time and space vanish as you become completely absorbed in a task. If you suddenly glance at a clock and exclaim, "It's been two hours already?!," you've likely been in a flow state. I was so engrossed in what I was doing that I didn't even notice the passing of time! "

Anyway, art is the best way to enter the flow state once you've overcome any self-criticism or frustration over not being able to draw "perfectly" (nothing is perfect — just love whatever you create!).

Some people prefer to simply create abstract colors or patterns, while others like to experiment with imaginative sketches of whatever comes to mind, and still others prefer to use a reference object, picture, or tutorial to help them with their creations. Any of those ways to begin drawing can help someone settle their breathing, calm their heartbeat, and enter a delicious state of meditation.

increased knowledge of what is possible.

Drawing anything serves as a reminder to the brain that anything is possible with enough imagination, resulting in a sense of freedom and delight.

Even though it's unlikely to see a man sitting in a tulip or a horseshoe crab riding a bike in the real world, it's still fun to imagine making them up on a blank piece of paper!

Laughter: For You and Others.

Speaking of smiles, it's a wonderful feeling to laugh at a work of art you've made, even if it's crude and silly. The cartoon whale and the ridiculous flower crown story had my kids and I in fits of laughter, which just goes to prove that you don't have to be a master illustrator to make people smile.

Parenting Support.

I'm constantly looking for family activities that will help us all bond as a multitasking mother. Drawing and the arts are suitable! And when I witness my kids' creativity in action, I feel awe and aww.

Creating Communities Can Help Banish Loneliness.

It can bring strangers together in a positive, mutually beneficial way, much like drawing ties families together. I recently learned about several Facebook groups where artists encourage one another, whether they are completely new to drawing or experienced.

These online groups can be found if you look around. A skilled moderator who upholds courtesy and respect is essential. You can also form your own group with friends who also want to start drawing discoveries (via text, online groups, etc.).

satisfaction with tangible results and discernible advancement.

Few things are as gratifying as looking at a well-made product and realizing, "I made this!

Drawing and art have the distinct advantage of creating PRODUCTS, or items that can be handled, displayed, and shared. That is satisfying!

The delicious sensation of seeing your own progress is another aspect of art that lends itself perfectly. Comparing your older artwork with newer pieces reveals the new techniques and superpowers you're developing, just as it's exciting to follow a workout regimen and see the tangible results of being able to lift more weight or run farther.

This brings us full circle to Benefit #1: Practicing drawing can result in increased confidence that translates from your art to your whole life! What might have previously seemed like a "mess-up" may turn out to be foreshadowing for a completely new direction your art takes!

Contents

Chapter 1 - Before you start drawing 1
   1.   You are harder on yourself than other people will be. 1
   2.   Step away if you need to. 1
   3.   The people online didn't get good overnight. 2
   4.   It's not speed painting. 2
   Pencil 3
   Eraser 3
   Sharpener 3
   Ruler 3
   Sketch Pad 3
   Smudge Sticks 4
   Work Space 4
   Comfortable Chair 4
   Good Light 4
   When you get serious 4
   T-Square 4
   Drafting Triangles 4
   Eraser Guard 5
   Kneaded Eraser 5
   Dry Cleaning Bag 5
   Horse Hair Brush 5
   Desk with Tilting Top 5

Chapter 2 – Fruits 6
   Cherry 6
   Plums 10

Chapter 3 - Everyday things 13
   Zippo 13
   Old Style Fan 19
   Stack of Books 22
   Alarm Clock 26

Jar	31
Chapter 4 – Plants	42
Buttercup	42
Lily	46
Office Chair	60
Desk Lamp	68
Chapter 6 – Animals	76
Lobster	80
Squirrel	83
Chapter 7 – Buildings	91
A Simple Shack	91
House	95
Chapter 8 - The Human Body	100
The Female Face	101
Female Body	108
Male Face	122
Male Body	128
Conclusion	138

Chapter 1 - Before you start drawing

We all get hyped up and excited when starting a new hobby or interest. We want to do it all, we want to do it right now and be great at it. We start out with high energy and often end up frustrated when it doesn't turn out the way we envisioned it. So, before you start, here are some nuggets of wisdom from someone who's been there.

1.   You are harder on yourself than other people will be.

Take a deep breath and keep telling yourself you are still learning. One problem we all face is hitting the ground running thinking it will be easy and when it's not, we beat ourselves up about the fact we can't grasp it. Take it easy on yourself. No one expects you to be Picasso out of the gate.

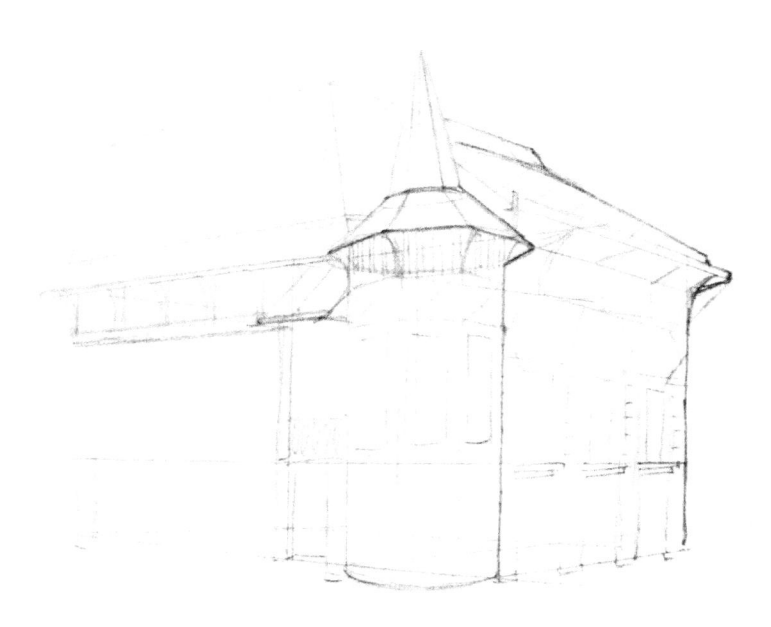

2.   Step away if you need to.

Take breaks when you feel the need, and sometimes if you don't. For every two hours you spend sitting and staring at the paper and drawing, you need to rest your eyes, mind, and exercise your body. Walk away from it and come back to your project in about 15 minutes.

3. The people online didn't get good overnight.

Some of us have the bad habit of comparing our work to the art we see online and getting mad or frustrated when it doesn't measure up to what we see. What we often forget is that the art we see online is the result of months and years of practicing techniques, pushing their limits and challenging themselves. It's best to compare the work you're doing now to the work you did when you first started out. You will see more a difference in your work and keep you on track and motivated.

4. It's not speed painting.

We've all seen speed paint videos and want to do that, but before you get the speed, you've got to get the techniques down and get used to strokes needed to make each piece of art. As your muscles get used to the strokes, you will get faster with your art.

I hope these tips for keeping your head in the game will come in handy. They do for me. Now, we go to the shopping list of things you will need to get started.

Your Basic List

Just starting out in a new hobby, you need to make sure you like it before you get all the tools you need to get started in it. Here are a few things you will most definitely need when getting your feet wet.

Pencil

This can be either a no. 2 pencil or a mechanical pencil. No need to get fancy with all the different types of lead that are available to you.

Eraser

A pink one is perfect.

Sharpener

There are many times you will need to draw a sharp, thin, line. Keeping this handy will be a life saver.

Ruler

This will help you draw your guide lines and also any straight lines will need to draw to keep things in order.

Sketch Pad

A sketch pad from any craft store or big box store will do. You don't need any of the fancy or really big ones just starting out.

Smudge Sticks

These are rolled pieces of paper that end in points. They are very useful when blending shadows.

Work Space

Any table in your home in which you can sit comfortably will do fine. This can be a tray table or dining room table.

Comfortable Chair

Any chair that lets you sit to where your feet can rest flat on the floor is perfect. You really don't need a fancy desk chair when you're just starting out.

Good Light

Most dining rooms have this, but in case your home doesn't have good lighting, a simple desk lamp with a soft white bulb will do fine.

When you get serious

This list is for when you find you like it and wants to step up to the next level.

T-Square

This is to help you place things like drafting triangles and rulers where you want them on the page. This tool is best suited for smaller desks.

Drafting Triangles

These come in 45-45-90 and 30-60-90 varieties and can help with drawing just the right angled lines for certain subjects.

Eraser Guard

This is a small thin piece of aluminum which has different types of holes in it. These holes help you erase the lines you don't want while keeping the lines need to have in the piece.

Kneaded Eraser

This eraser is gray and is easily molded and ripped apart. This eraser is used to lighten shading, smudge pencil marks and also to add highlights in pictures.

Dry Cleaning Bag

This is a bag filled with eraser shavings. You can shake it on your work surface to help prevent smudging.

Horse Hair Brush

This tool is used to sweep your work clean without smudging it.

Desk with Tilting Top

This is a good upgrade to a dining room table. Tilting your work space reduces bending over it to draw.

Chapter 2 – Fruits

We are going to start with the most basic of subjects to sketch, things that don't move. As I walk you through the steps, I will also add in explanations about shading and shading techniques.

Cherry

There are a few things to take note here. Don't look at the cherry as a whole. Look at its individual shapes and name the shapes. This way you are looking at the parts to the whole and not the whole piece. Our logical mind wants to classify and name what we see; often giving the illusion that drawing something is harder than it actually is.

1. Draw two overlapping circles.

2. Draw two curved lines from each of the circles.

3. Draw a small rectangle at the top to join the two stems.

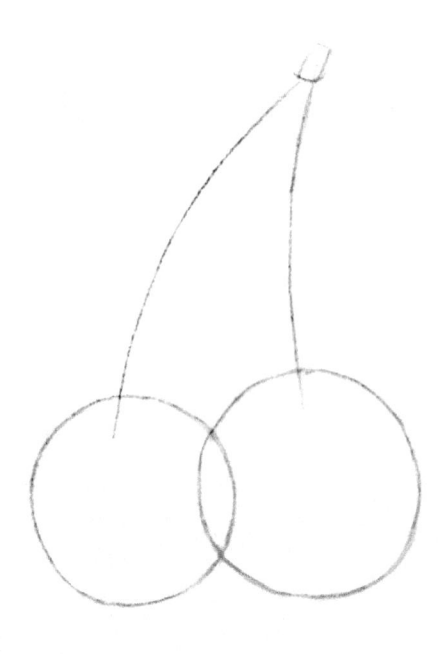

4. Draw a second set of curved lines.

5. Draw thick lines inside the rectangle for the bumps.

6. Darken the lines and use your finger to smudge them a bit for the shaded effect.

7. Draw a curved line from the stem on the right to the edge of the circle to create the bump you see in the picture.

8. Holding your pencil at an angle, make light strokes going across the front of both cherries. Take note of the places where there is no light. This is where the light source is hitting the cherry the most.

9. To darken, shade over those places again.

Things to note:

-There are shaded places on the top of the cherry. This is how you shade for depth and effect.

10. Keep layering the shading technique until you get the effect you see on the cherries.

11. Use the same technique to shade under the cherries, but use your finger to smudge it so that the shadow is smoother.

Plums

This is a slightly oblong shape and will take a little more practice to get right. You can, if you wish, purchase an ellipse template from a craft or drafting store to help you, but the shape does not have to be perfect.

1. Draw the oblong shapes so they overlap.

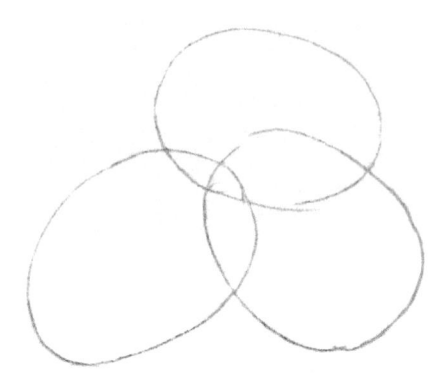

2. Use the curve technique from the cherry here on the plums.

3. Draw your stems as curved lines that meet at the end.

4. Draw a rounded rectangle for the leaf.

5. Draw curved quick lines for the shading of the plums. This is called contour shading.

6. Add a jagged edge to the leaf.

7. Darken the shading in the places you see in the picture.

8. Add the shadows under the fruit like you did with the cherries.

Extra Practice

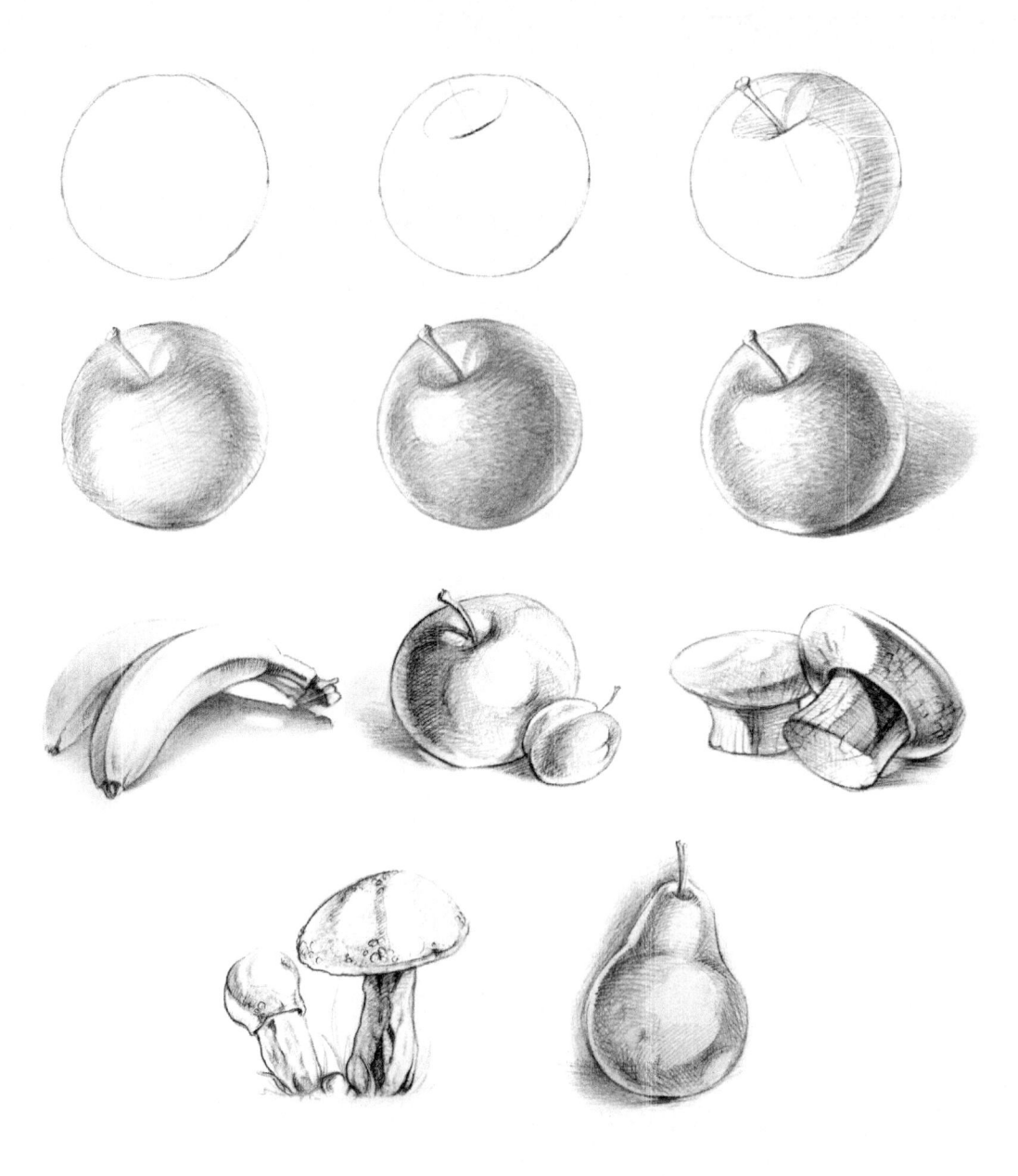

Chapter 3 - Everyday things

It's the little things that can make a drawing, and getting them just right can make a picture have a more realistic feel.

Zippo

Things to note:

-The shading will be slightly different to depict the shiny metal of the lighter.

- The flint wheel is darker to depict the color of the wheel in contrast to the rest of the lighter.

1. Draw a slight trapezoid.

2. Draw a "T" in the shape.

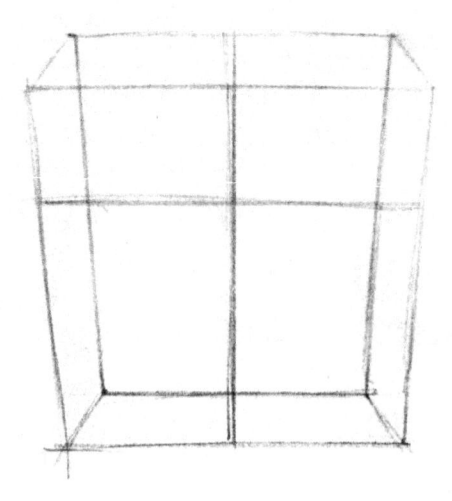

3. Draw the lines back to the rear of the shape.
4. Connect the lines to make the 3d look.
5. Draw the second cross bar under the first.
6. Draw the cube on the right-top of the space.

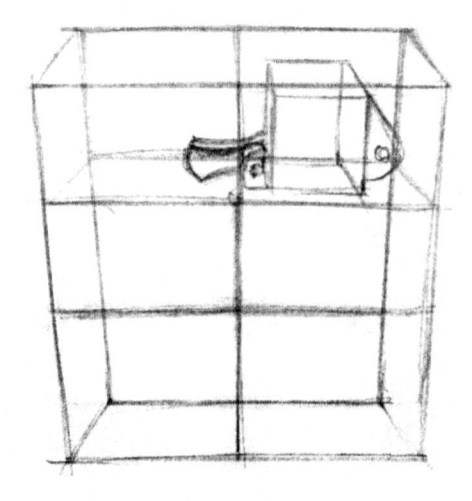

7. Draw a diagonal line coming from the right of the cube.

8. Add the curve and the small circle to the diagonal line.

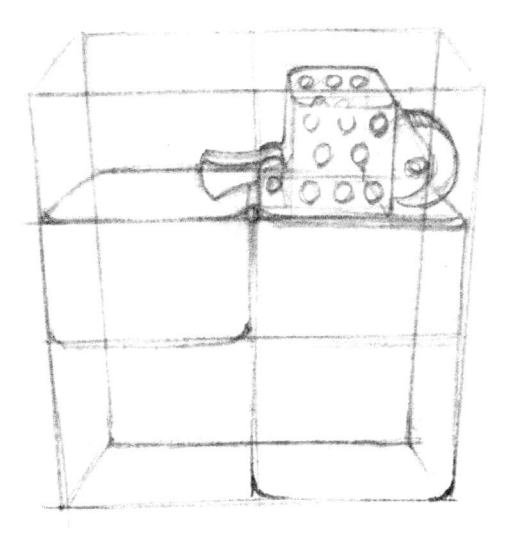

9. Draw two curves that almost touch one another.
10. Add the curve at the end of the first two.
11. Add the little curve and small circle in front of the arm.
12. Draw a second small curve behind the arm to make it look 3d.
13. Draw the curved lines for the top and the bottom of the case.
14. Draw the small circles on the vent.
15. Draw 3/4 of a circle for the flint wheel.

16. Draw a curve behind the circle.

17. Erase your guide lines.

18. Shade the inside of the cap.

19. Shade the wheel.

20. Shade where the vent sits.

21. Shade the inside of the vent.

22. Make the small inner line where the vent sits.

23. Make an inner line to make the bevel for the case.

24. Make a light distinction line 3/4 of the way down the lighter.

25. To shade the case, first make your quick strokes horizontal. Then, go back over another set of quick lines diagonal over the first.

Take this time to compare what you have done to the picture above. Add anything you may have missed.

26. Add more layers to the initial shading to darken it in the places you see in the picture.

27. Add the shadow at the base of the Zippo.

Old Style Fan

1. Make a triangle with a rounded edge.

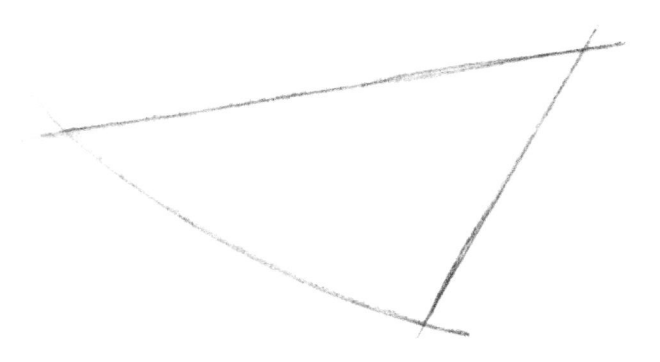

2. Draw the rays of the fan.

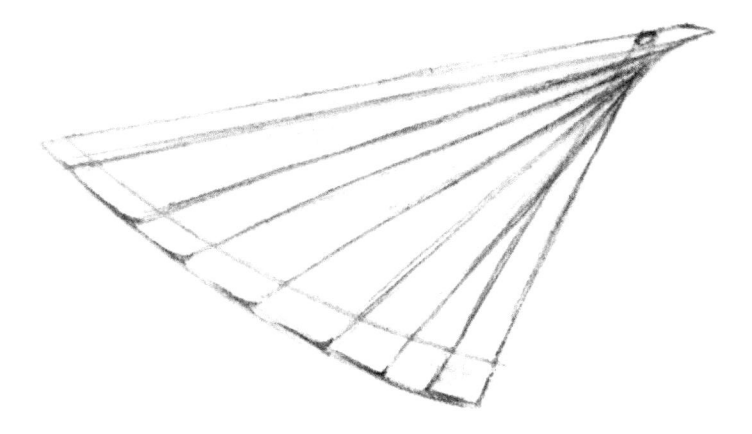

3. Add the small circle in the back.
4. Draw a secondary curve inside the first.

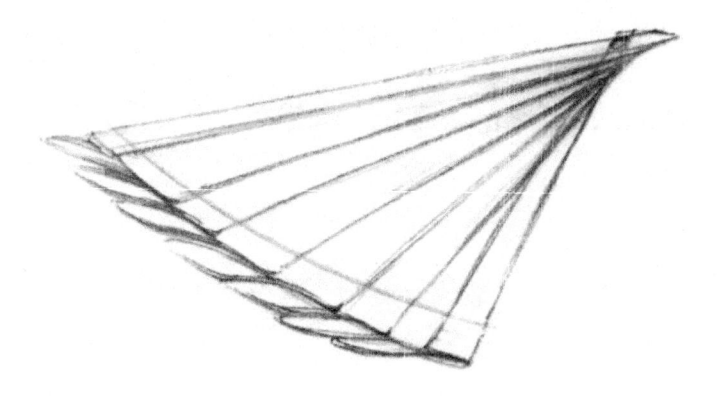

5. Darken the areas you see in the picture to start your shading.

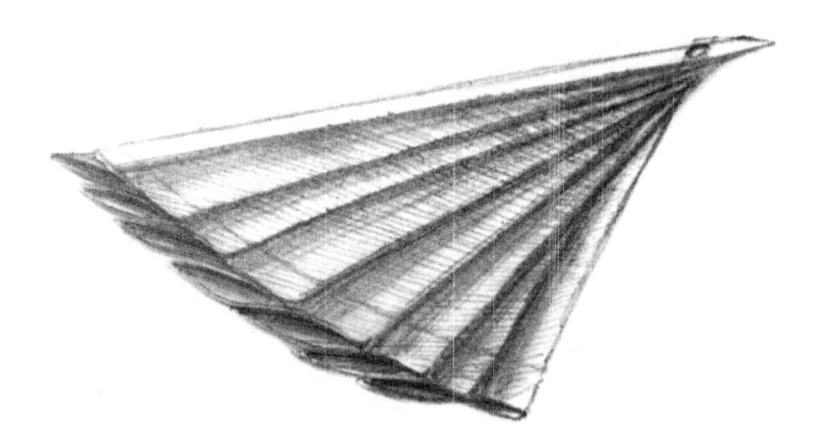

6. Draw tear drops under each ray to make the pleats.
7. Add your contour shading.

8. Use your finger and light strokes with your eraser to get the effect you see in the picture above.

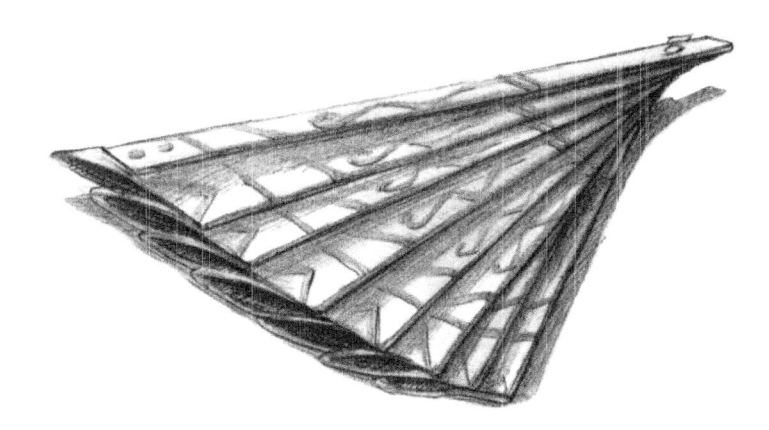

9. Add the decorations you see and tweak the shading as needed.

Stack of Books

1. Draw your cube.

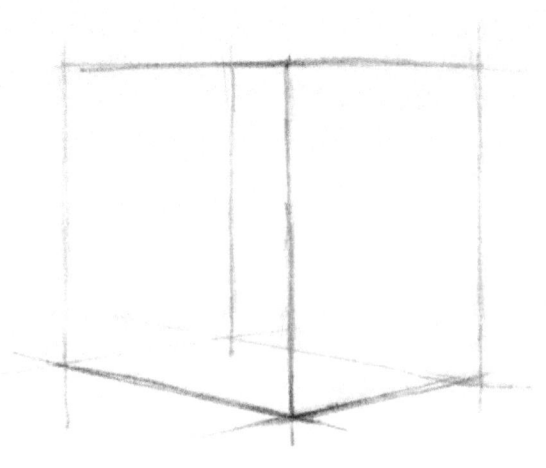

2. Draw the lines to distinguish between the books.

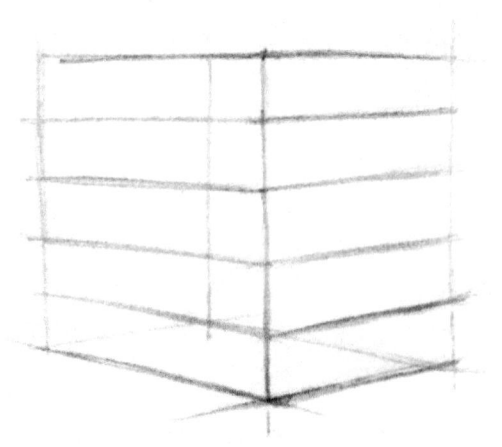

3. Add the lines in the rear of the cube.

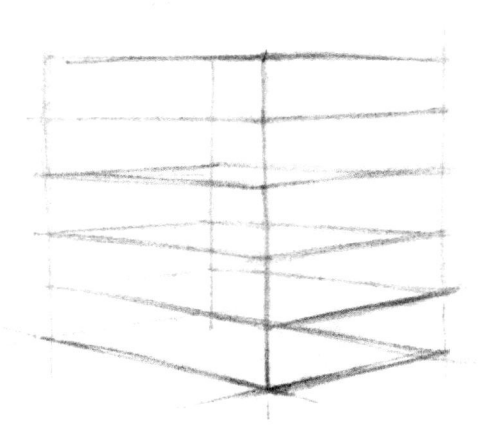

4. Draw the curves for the book spines and pages.

5. Add the double lines for the book covers.

6. Erase the lines to clean up the picture.
7. Add the spine decorations for the books.
8. Draw the thin lines for the pages.
9. Shade in the stack.

10. Refine your shading of the stack.

Alarm Clock

1. Draw the slanted square you see.

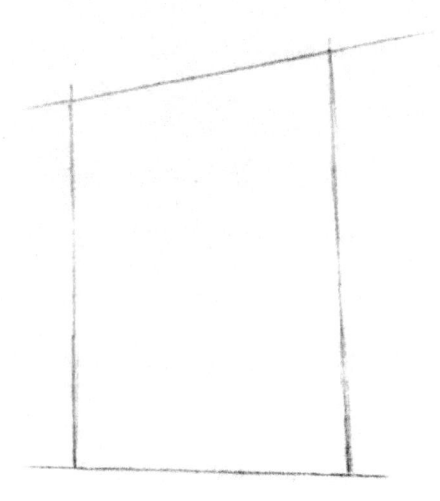

2. Add to the square as you see in the picture.

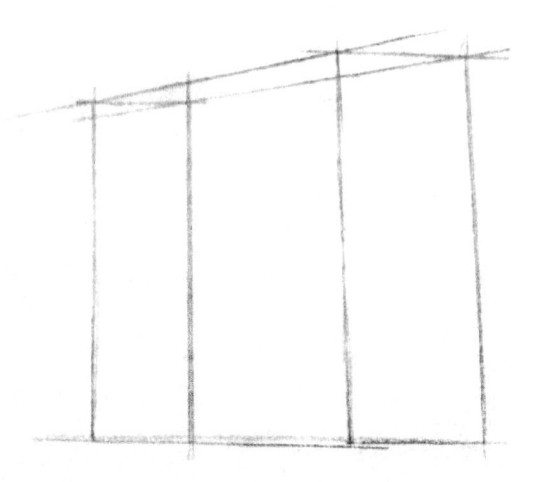

3. Add the "T"s in the picture before you do anything else.
4. Draw the circles according to the quadrants you've just made.

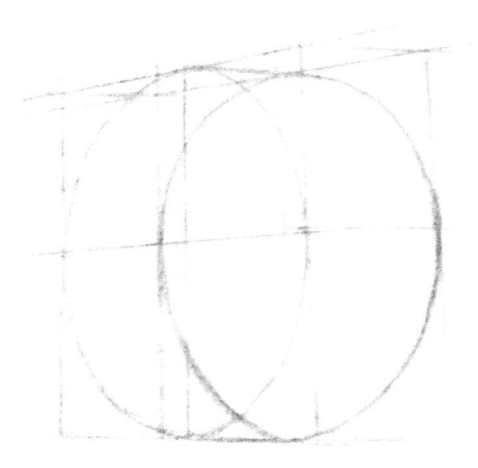

5. Add the line at the top which connects the two circles.
6. Erase the guides.

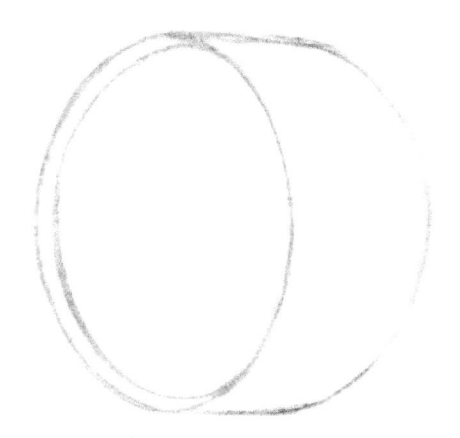

7. Draw the inside curve.

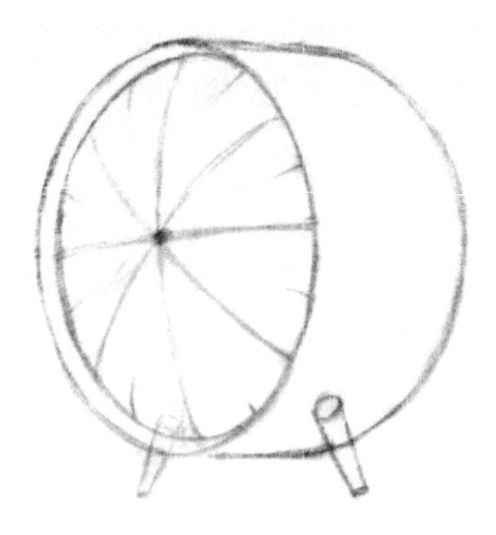

8. Add the dot in the middle.
9. Draw curved lines coming from the center.
10. Add the legs.

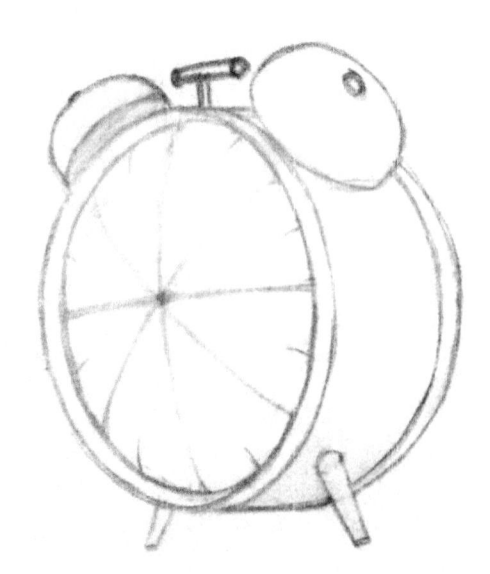

11. Draw the "T" at the top for the hammer.

12. Draw the curves before you finish the bells.
13. Draw domes to finish the bells.
14. Add the circles at the top of the bells.
15. Add the black spots on the face.
16. Draw the circle to link the spots.
17. Add your numbers.

18. Erase the rays you had for guides.
19. Use the same shading technique you did with the Zippo here.
20. Add the hands.
21. Add the shading you see in the picture.

Compare what you've done so far to the picture above. Add anything you don't have on your page.

Jar

1. Draw cylinder you see in the picture.

2. Draw a circle at the base of the jar.
3. Draw the curve for the handle.
4. Draw the curves for the neck of the jar.
5. Draw the ellipse inside the jar.
6. Add the base for the jar.

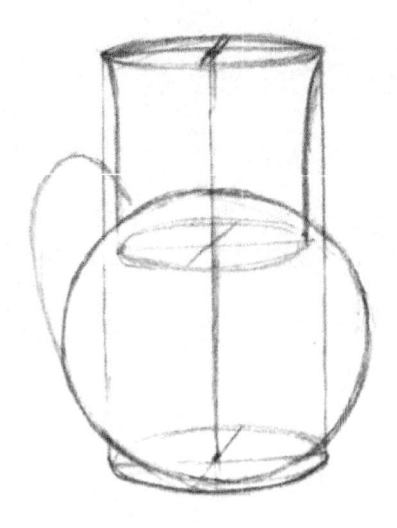

7. Draw a dome on the top of the jar.
8. Add the part on the top.
9. Lightly contour shade the jar.

10. Add the curves for the handle.

11. Add the semi-circle at the base of each of the places for the handle.

12. Continue the shading.

13. Take your pencil and eraser to create the shiny and shaded areas in the picture.

14. Add the decorations you see in the picture.

15. Keep using the technique from step 13 until you get the shading you see on the left.

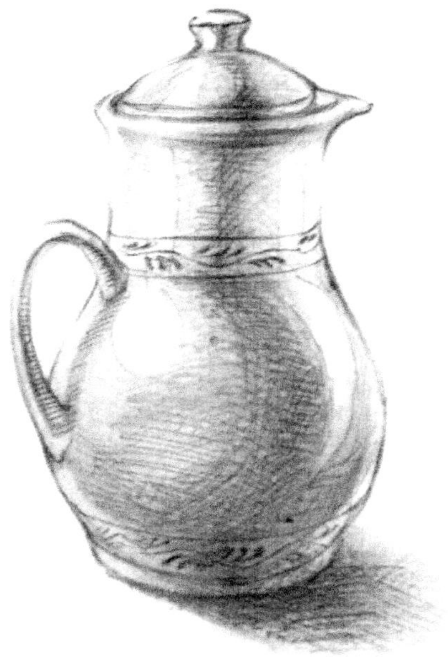

Extra Practice

37

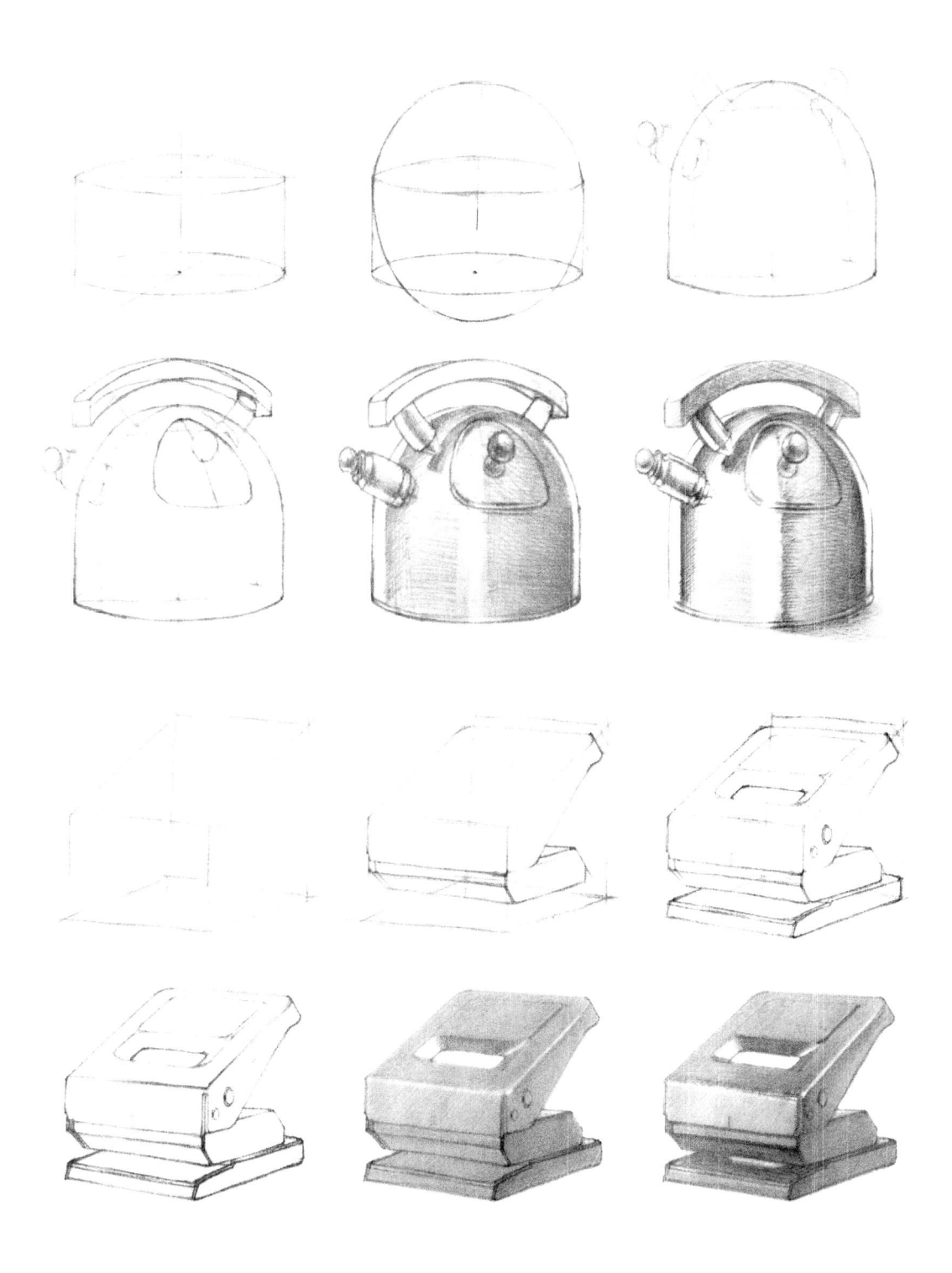

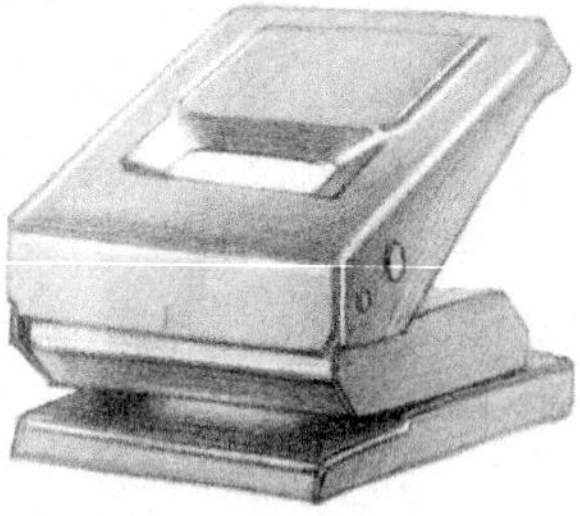

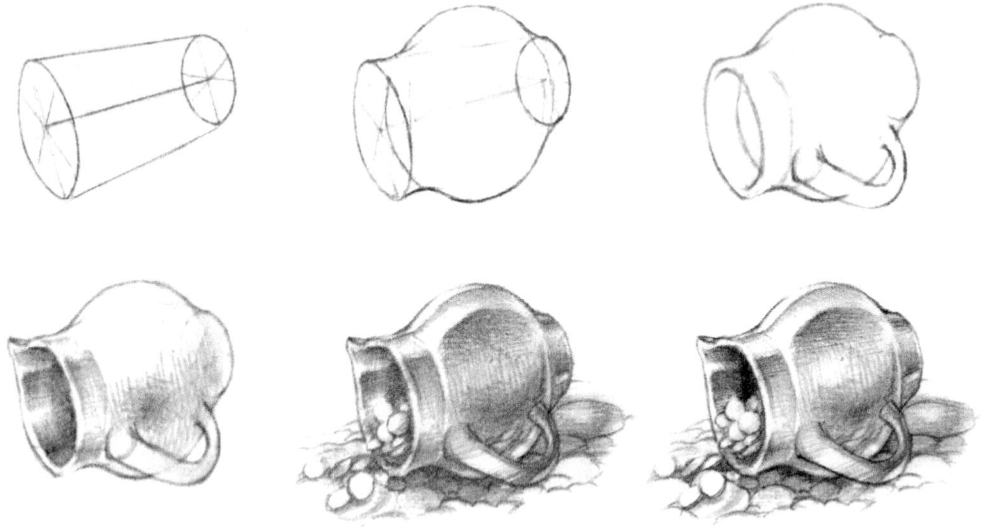

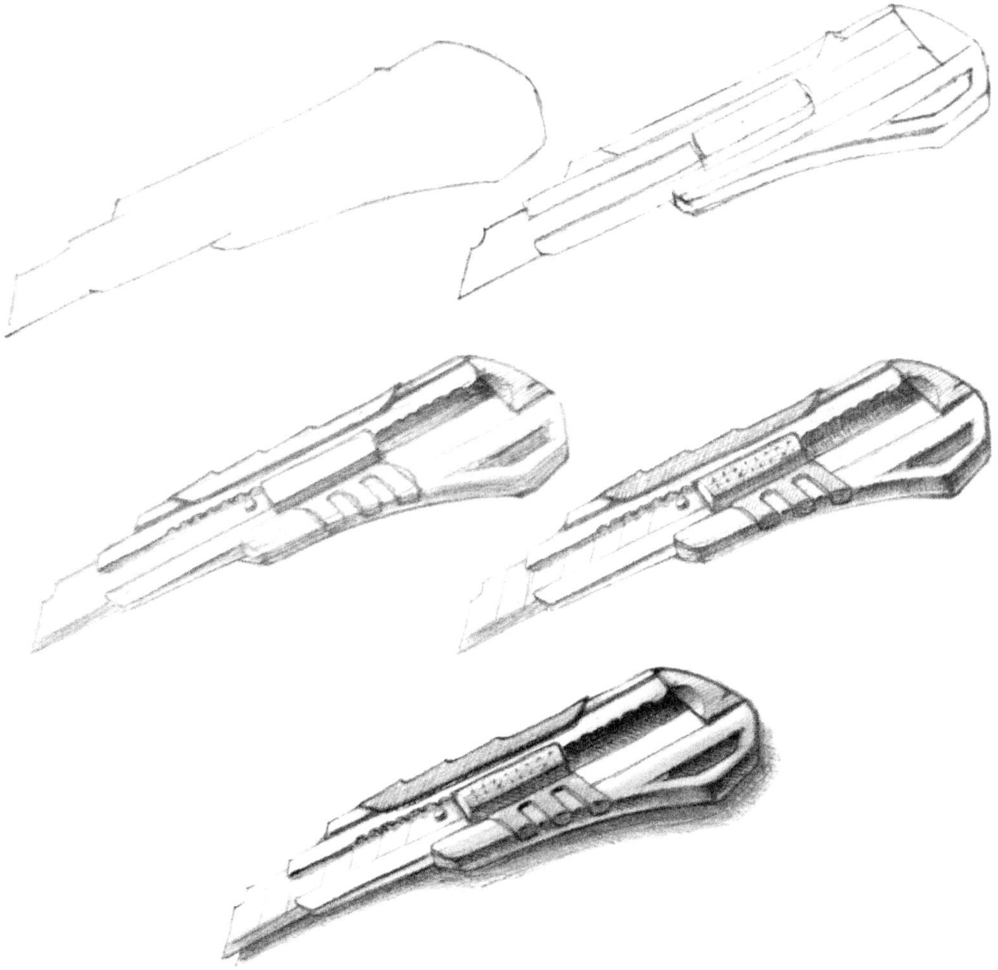

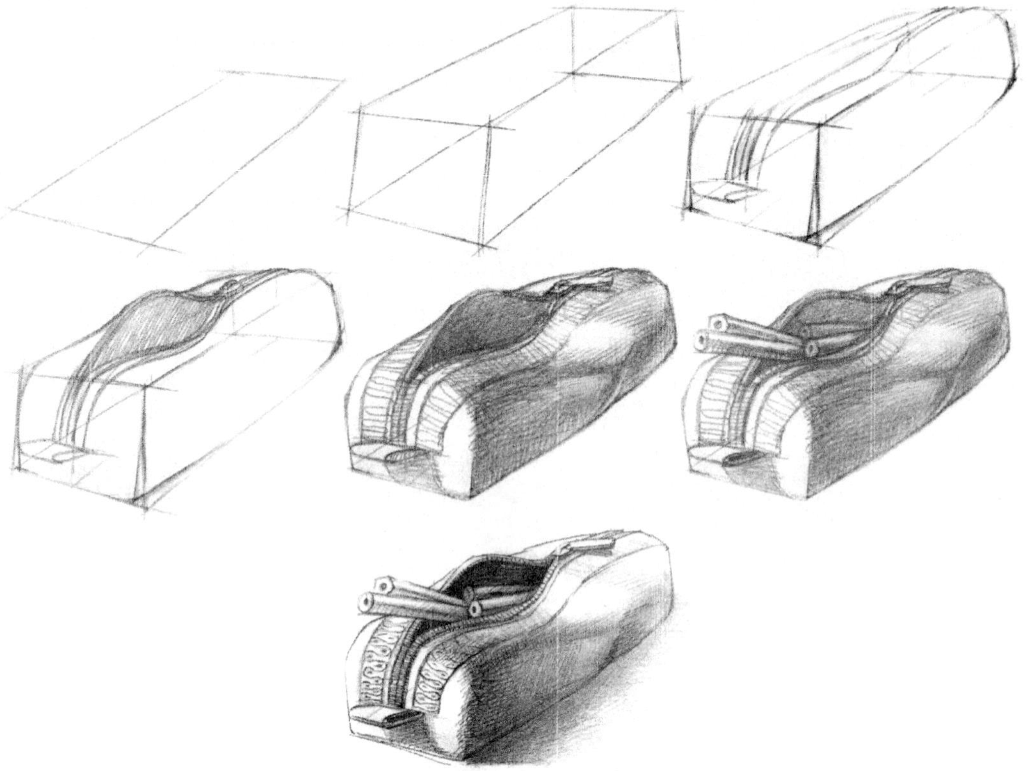

41

Chapter 4 – Plants

There are many flowers in the world. Here is just two of them, but don't stop with just these. Take pictures of many different flowers and practice drawing them.

Buttercup

1. Draw your line to depict the ground.
2. Draw the curved "V" for the leaves.
3. Draw the stem.

4. Draw the circle for the bloom.

5. Draw the long loops for the leaves.
6. Draw a circle for the middle of the bloom.
7. Draw the jagged edges around the circle.

8. Draw the smaller circle in the center of the bloom.
9. Draw the tear drop shapes for the petals.
10. Draw the line just under the bloom for the bump on the stem.
11. Start adding your shading.

Compare what you have drawn to this picture before you continue shading. Add in anything that has been left out.

12. Finish the shading.

Lily

1. Draw the ellipse for the pad.
2. Draw the three steps coming up from the pad.
3. Draw the ellipses at the top of the stems.

4. Add the smaller ellipse.
5. Draw the curved lines for the leaves on the ground.
6. Draw the smaller flower.
7. Draw the crooked curves for the smaller flowers.
8. Draw rounded petals for the large flower.

9. Start your shading.

10. Erase the lines you've used for the guides to help you draw the flowers and leaves.

11. Finish shading the picture.

Extra Practice

Chapter 5 - Home and Office

There are many pieces of furniture that make up a home. Here are some lessons on how to draw them, with some for you to do on your own.

1. Draw a square at an angle.

2. Draw a cube.

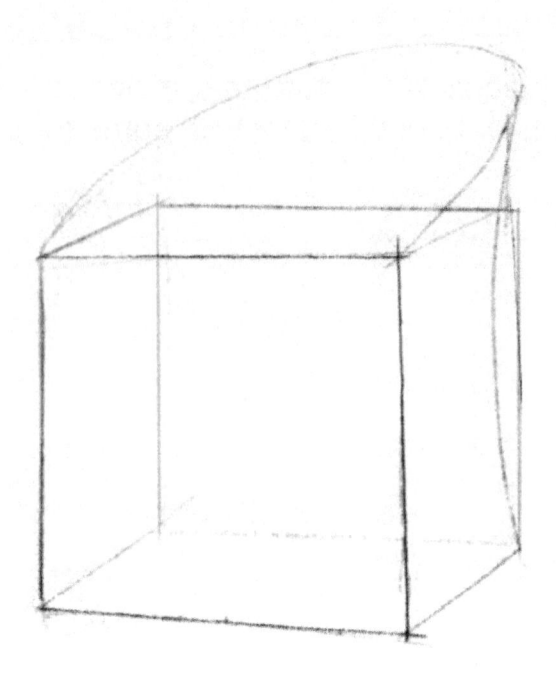

3. Draw the curve from corner to corner as in the picture.
4. Draw the curve on the rear, right side.
5. Draw the two flat squares you see in the picture.

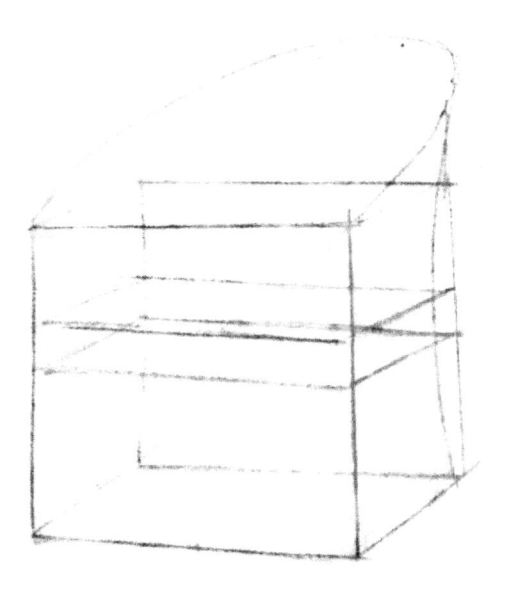

6. Draw the curves for the front legs.
7. Draw the curve on the front of the chair.
8. Draw the back legs.

9. Round out the cushion.

10. Make a faint line for the back of the chair.

11. Erase the guide lines.

Compare what you have done so far. Add in anything you haven't yet.

12. We are still cleaning up the chair in this step.

13. Start the shading by using cross-hatching.

14. Add the adornments you see in the picture.

15. Add the rest of the decorations on the chair.

16. Add the shading to finish the picture.

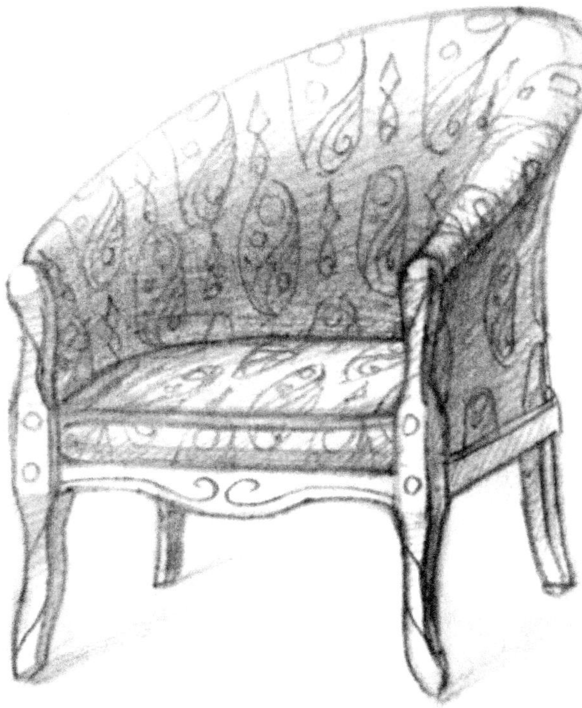

Office Chair

1. Draw two ellipses.
2. Draw a line bisecting the ellipses.
3. Draw the lines connection them.

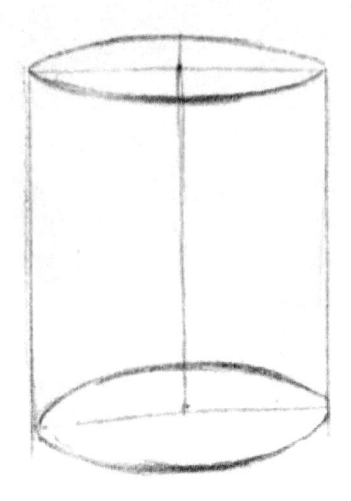

4. Draw the star pattern on the bottom ellipse.
5. Draw a square around the top ellipse.

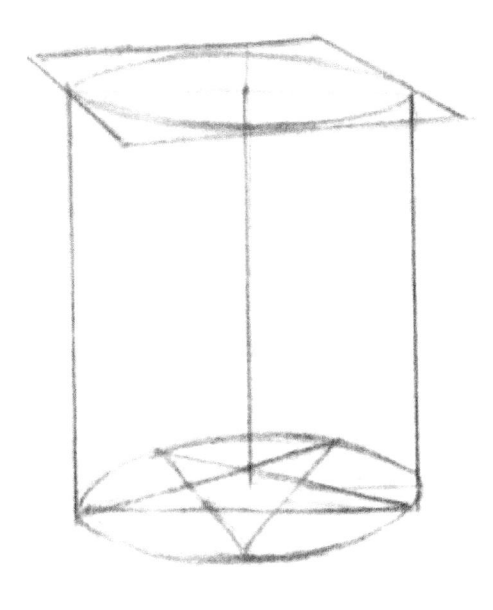

6. Draw the curves for the cushion of the chair.

7. Connect the curves.
8. Turn the star into rays.
9. Draw another ellipse under the one with the rays.

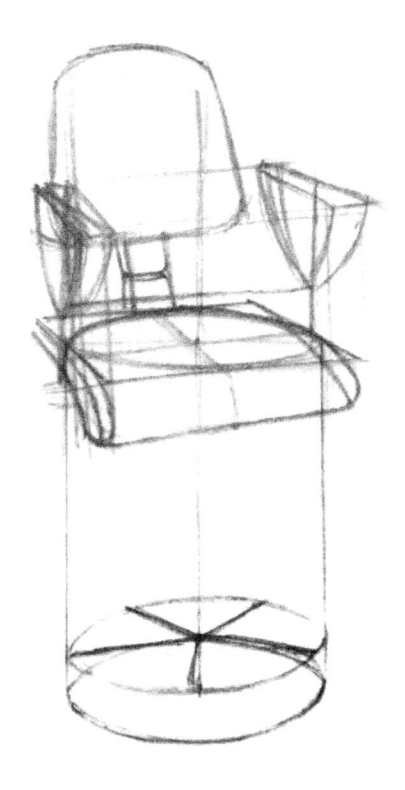

10. Draw the curved squares for the back support.
11. Draw rounded triangles for the armrest.
12. Double the arm rest up to make it wider.
13. Draw a rounded trapezoid for the back cushion.

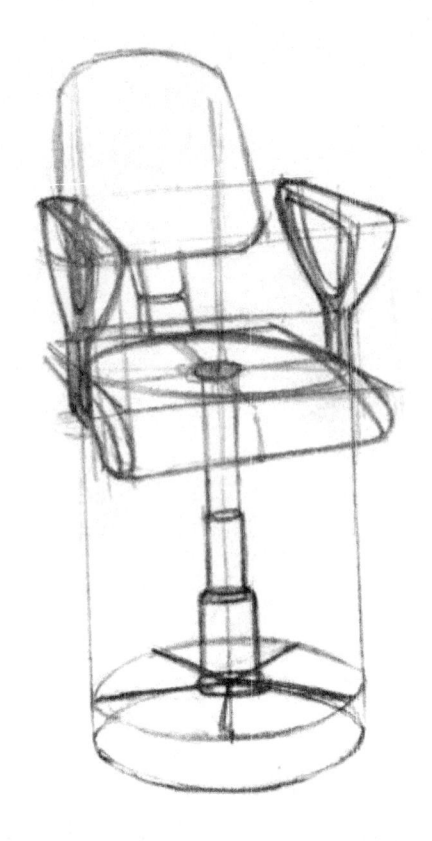

14. Draw a small, dark ellipse in the center of the seat.
15. Add the graduated curves for the support of the chair.
16. Draw the lines from the armrest to the seat.

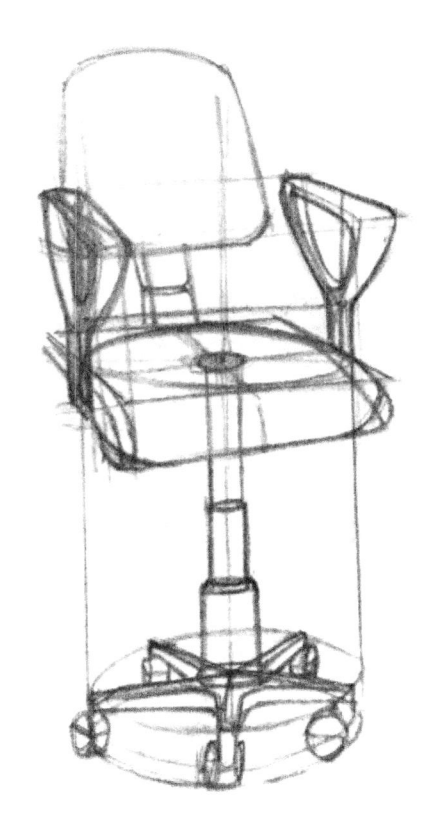

17. Draw the curves to decorate the arms of the base of the office chair.

18. Draw the circles for the wheels.

19. For the wheels you can't see, draw curves on the wheels.

20. Erasing all the guide lines.

Take this time to compare how far you've come in the lesson, adding in any details you may have left out.

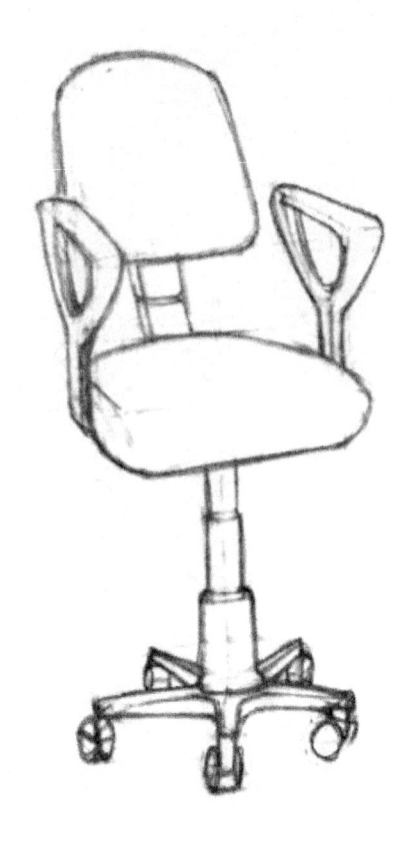

21. Make cross-hatch marks for the upholstery.
22. Draw contour marks on the base.
23. Darken the rest of the picture as you see it.
24. Add the arm under the seat.
25. Copy the shading you see in the picture to finish the chair.

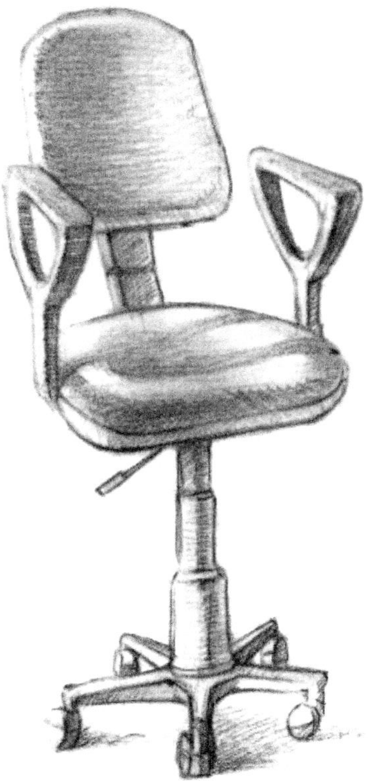

Desk Lamp

1. Draw an ellipse.
2. Draw a curve going down to the base.

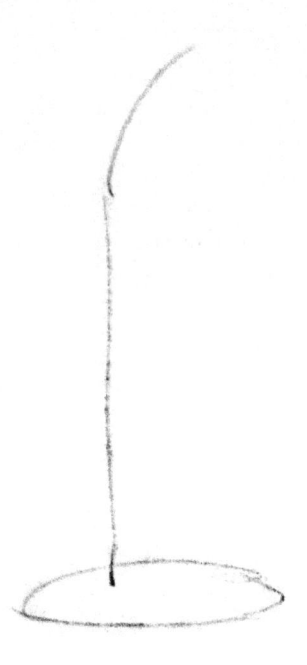

3. Draw a small ellipse above the curve.

4. Draw another ellipse diagonally under the first.
5. Draw a line from smaller one connecting to the larger one.
6. Draw another ellipse under the base.

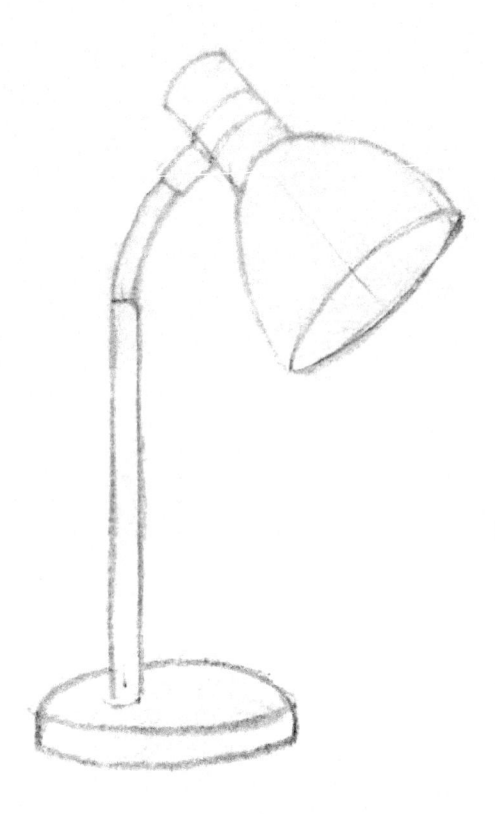

7. Draw an angled "U" for the shade of the lamp.
8. Draw a rectangle coming from the shade.
9. Draw the lines on the rectangle.
10. Add the extra lines in the picture to further flesh out the lamp.

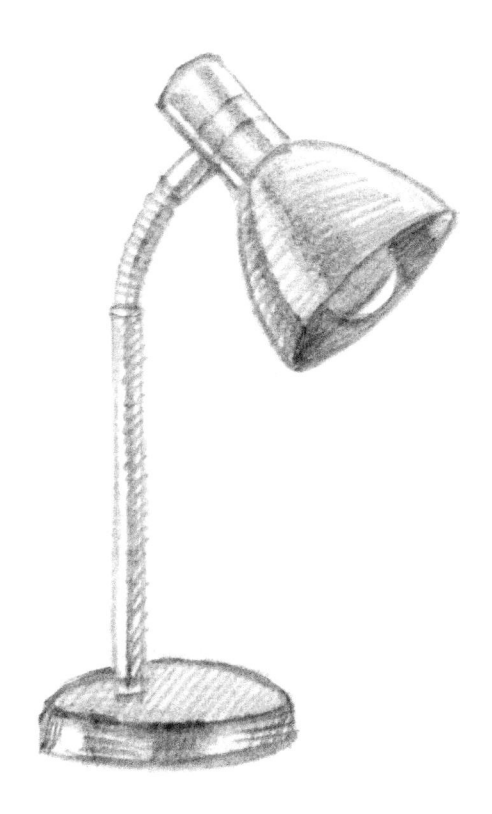

11. Using contour shading, fill in the lamp.

12. Use selective erasing to make the shiny parts of the lamp.

Take note of the lines added for the adjustable neck of the lamp.

13. Add the rest of the shading you see in the picture.

Extra Practice

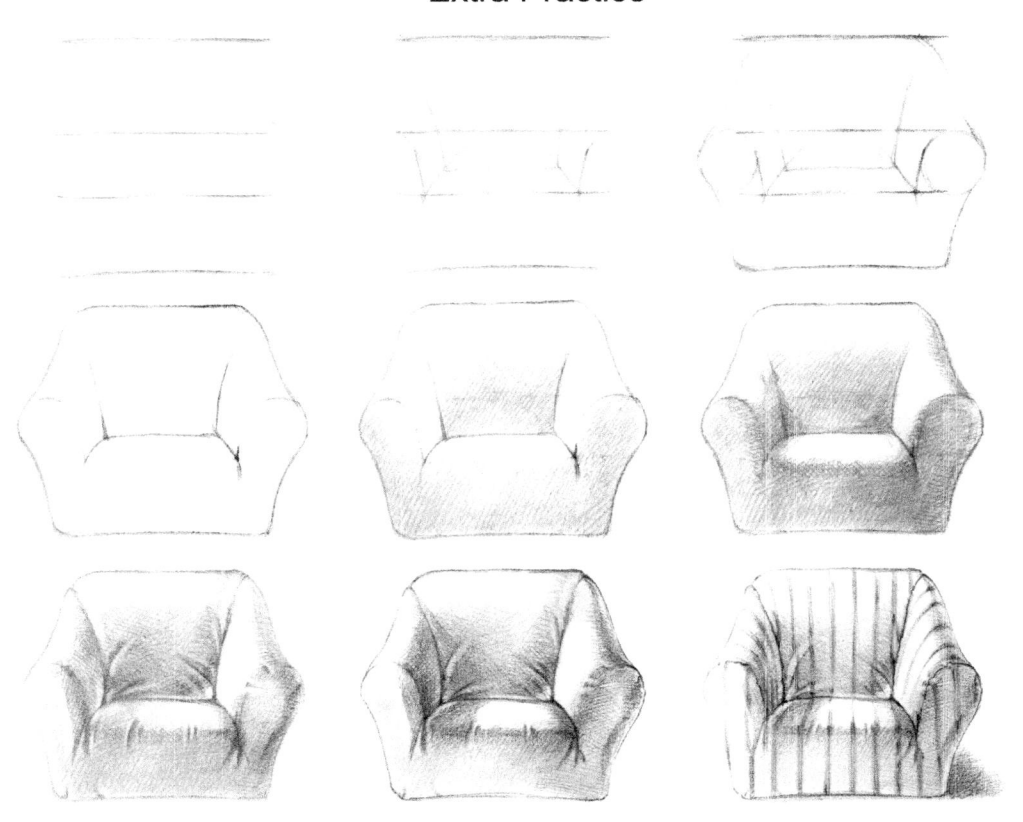

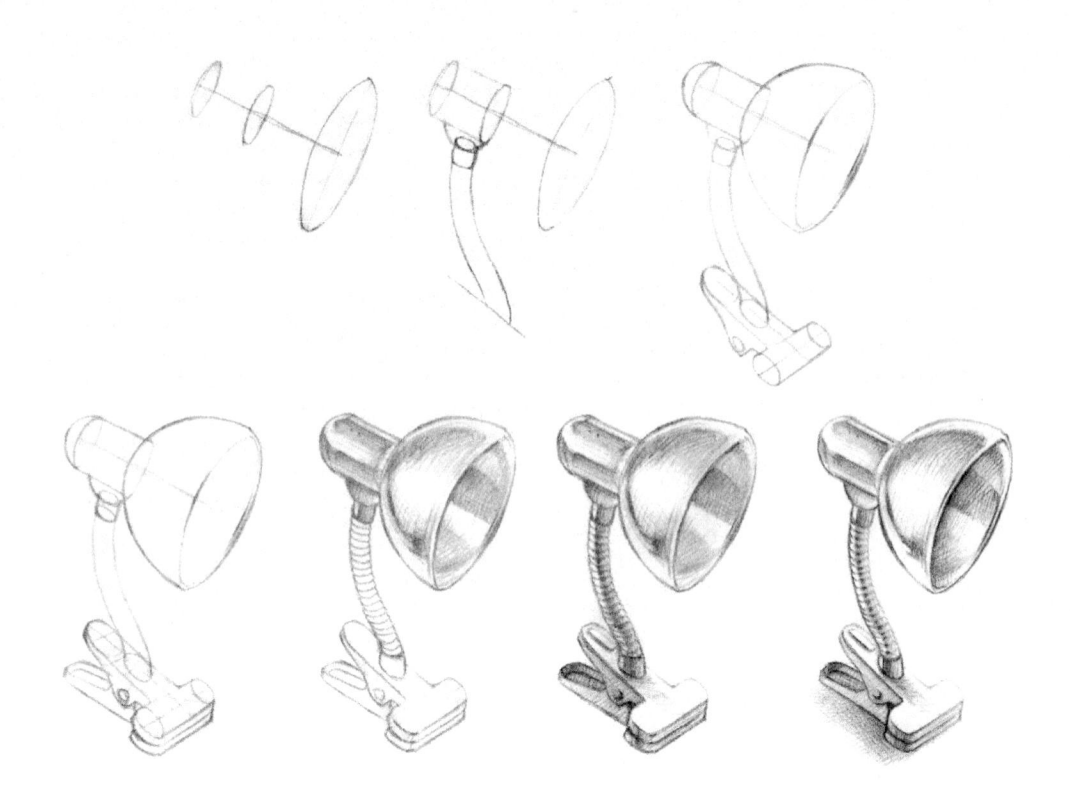

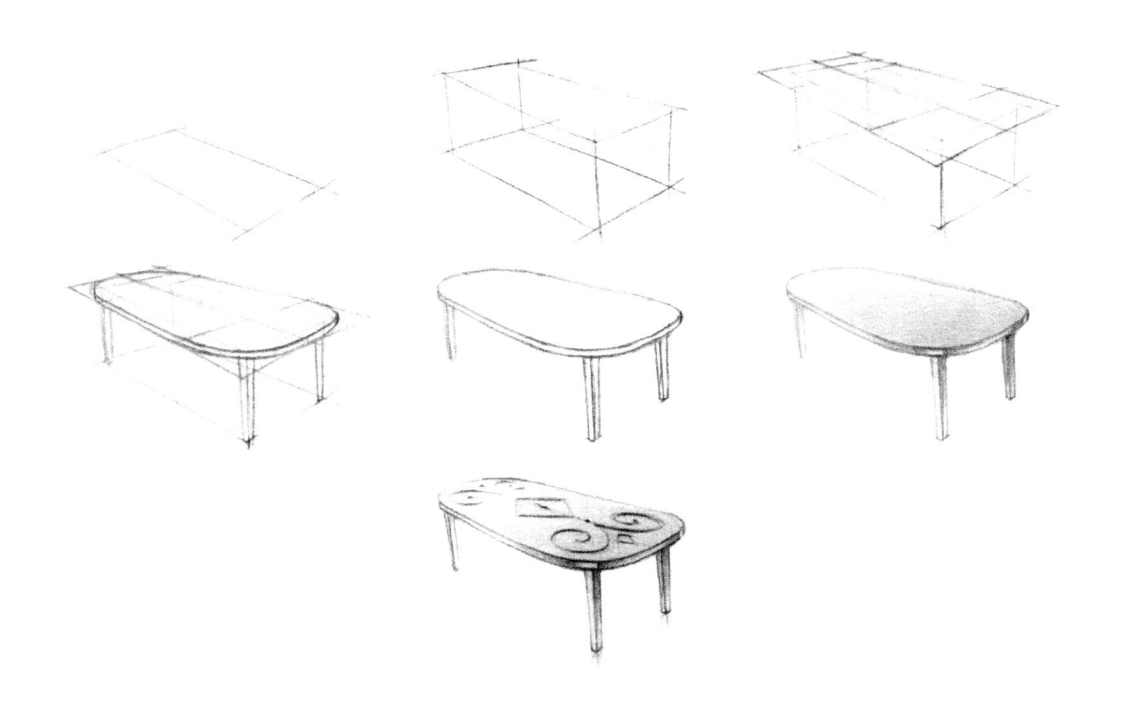

Chapter 6 – Animals

We're starting out with fish and moving up.

1. Draw a rounded triangle on its side.
2. Draw the guide lines you see on the triangle.
3. Draw the curve for the dorsal fin.
4. Draw the curvy line coming down from the dorsal.

5. Draw the long sweeping curves for the tail.
6. Draw the "J" shape for the eye on the right.
7. Draw another "J" for the eye on the left.
8. Draw the curves for the mouth and part under it.

9. Draw the front fins by making the curves first.

10. Using long, flowing strokes fill in the fins.

11. Draw the parts under the fish.

12. Draw the circles inside the eyes.

13. Add the lines above the mouth.
14. Add the lines for the tongue and the dots above the mouth.
15. Make small curves for the scales.
16. Shade in as shown.

Lobster

1. Draw the large ellipse for the body.
2. Draw the smaller ellipses around the larger one.
3. Draw the loose triangle for the pincer.

4. Draw the lines coming from the front of the ellipse.
5. Add the eye.

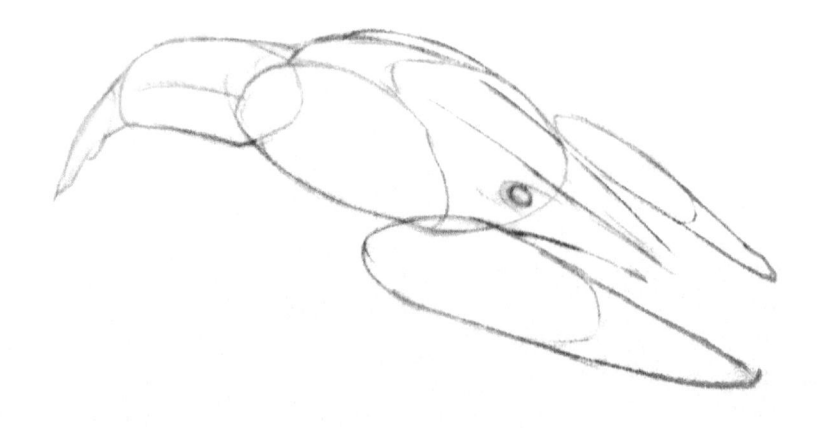

6. Finish the pincers.

7. Draw the curve for the tail.

Add in any details you haven't yet.

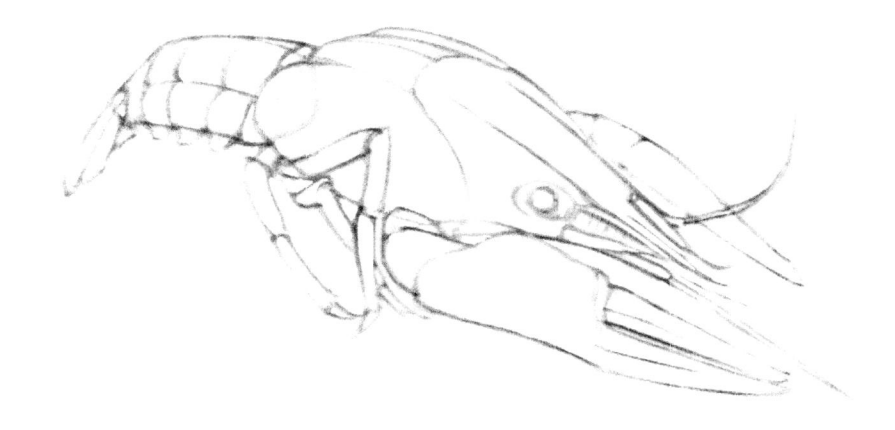

8. Shape the pincer closest to you. Do this by draw the lines and curves starting from the top and working your way down.

9. Rounded rectangles make up the legs.

10. Draw curves for the mouth and antennae.

11. Draw the lines on the tail.

12. Add lines to the very end of the tail.

Add in any lines and details you haven't yet.

13. Shade in as you see in the picture above.

Squirrel

1. Draw the circle for the head.
2. Add curves for the body.
3. Add another set of curves for the tail.
4. More curves make the hands and light details on the tail.

5. Darken the area around the nose and sharpen it a bit.
6. Draw an ellipse for the eye.
7. Draw the curve for the lower jaw.
8. Add the ears.
9. Add the curves for the arms.
10. Add the curves for the feet.

11. Darken the back slightly.

Take this time to compare what you have done this far before you continue. Add in any details you may have left out.

12. Using quick strokes make the fur effect.
13. Use longer strokes for the whiskers.
14. Add the pupil for the eye.
15. Add the nostrils.
16. Darken the places around the ears and belly.
17. Draw the jagged lines for the ground.
18. Add short curved lines for the feet and fingers.
19. Finish the shading as you see in the picture.

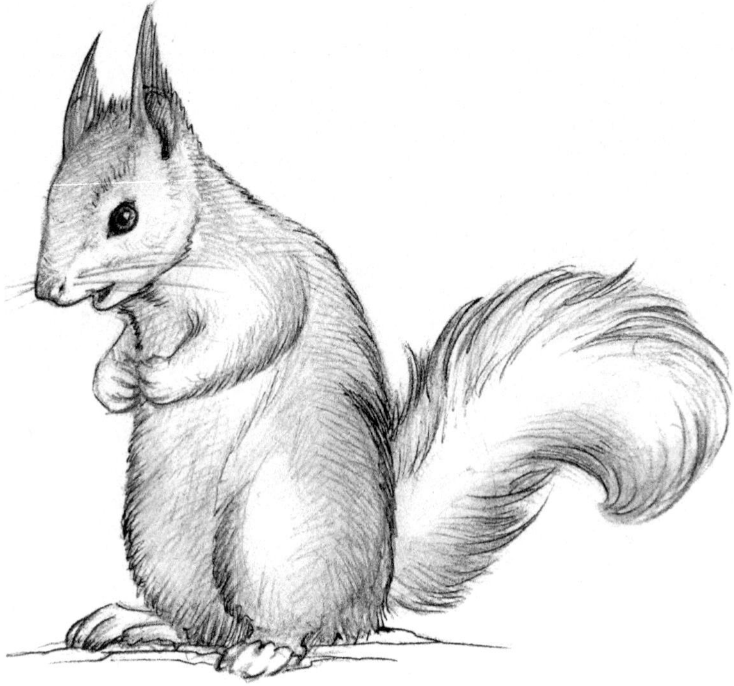

Extra Practice

89

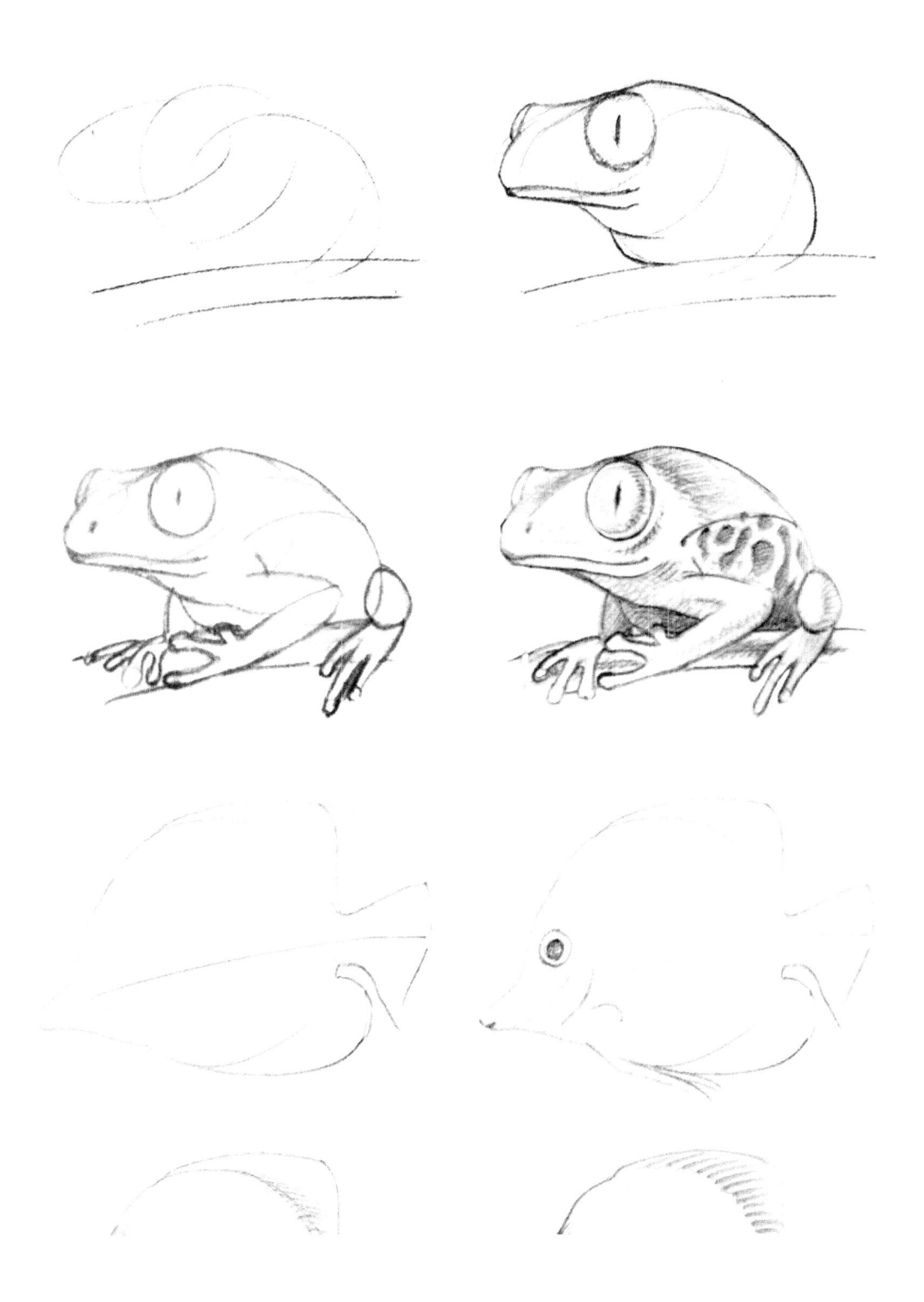

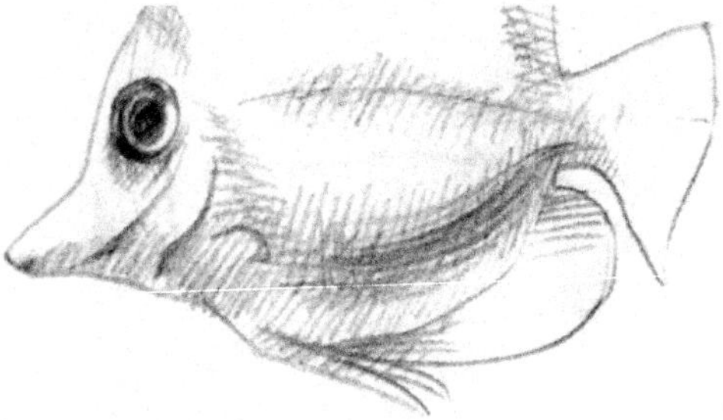
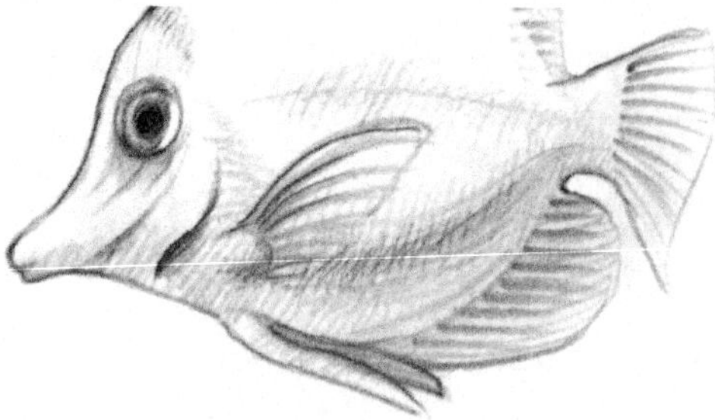
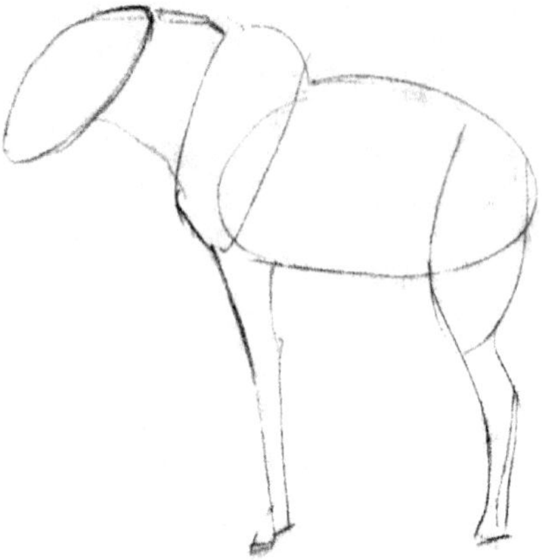
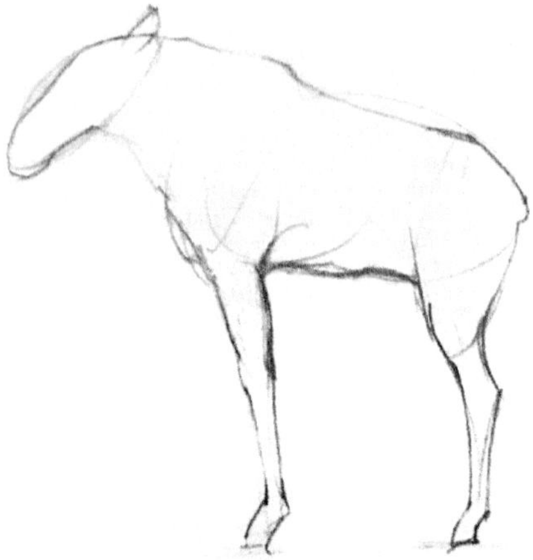
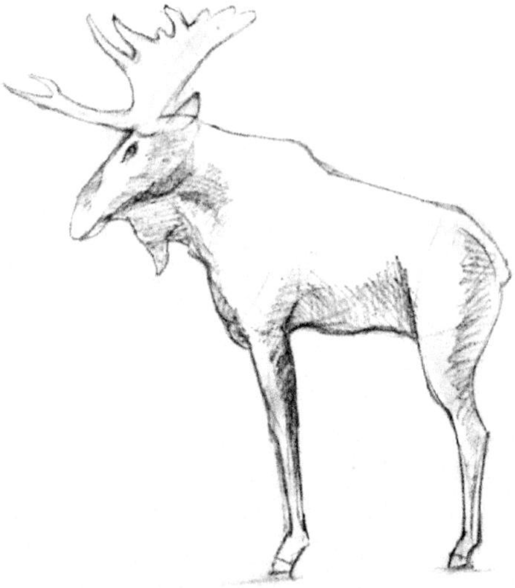
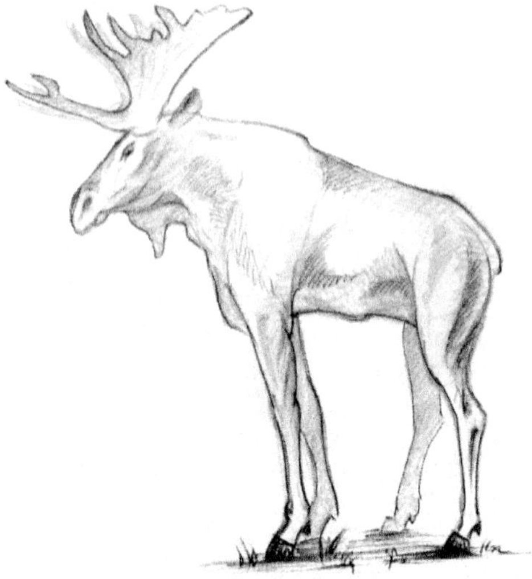

Chapter 7 – Buildings

There are different types of buildings and we will introduce a few here.

A Simple Shack

1. Take a ruler and make the lines you see in the picture.

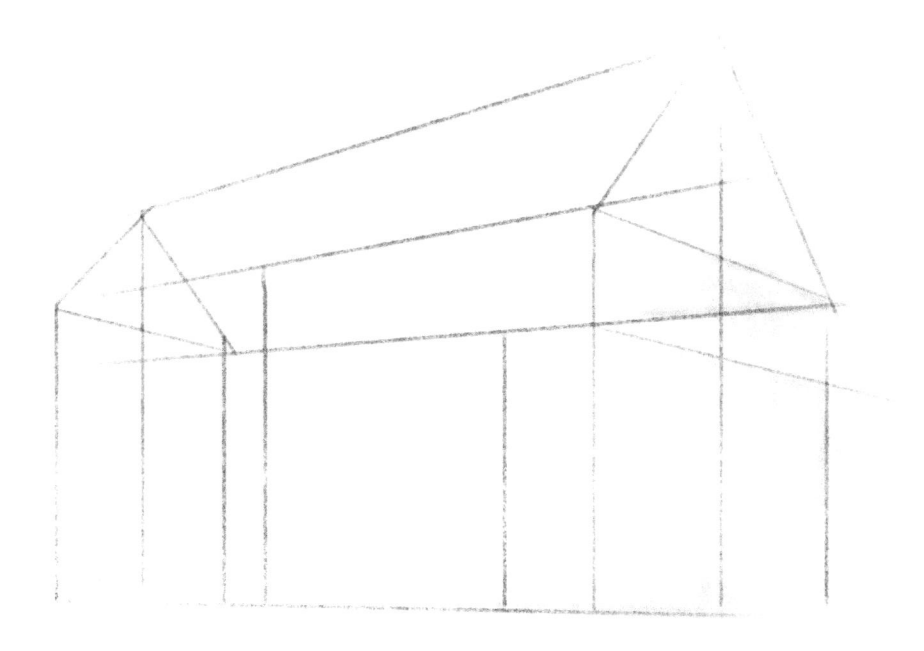

2. Taking your ruler, draw the shingles on the top of the shack.
3. Also, take the same ruler and make a slanted front for the shack,
4. Fill in the rest of the details with just your pencil.

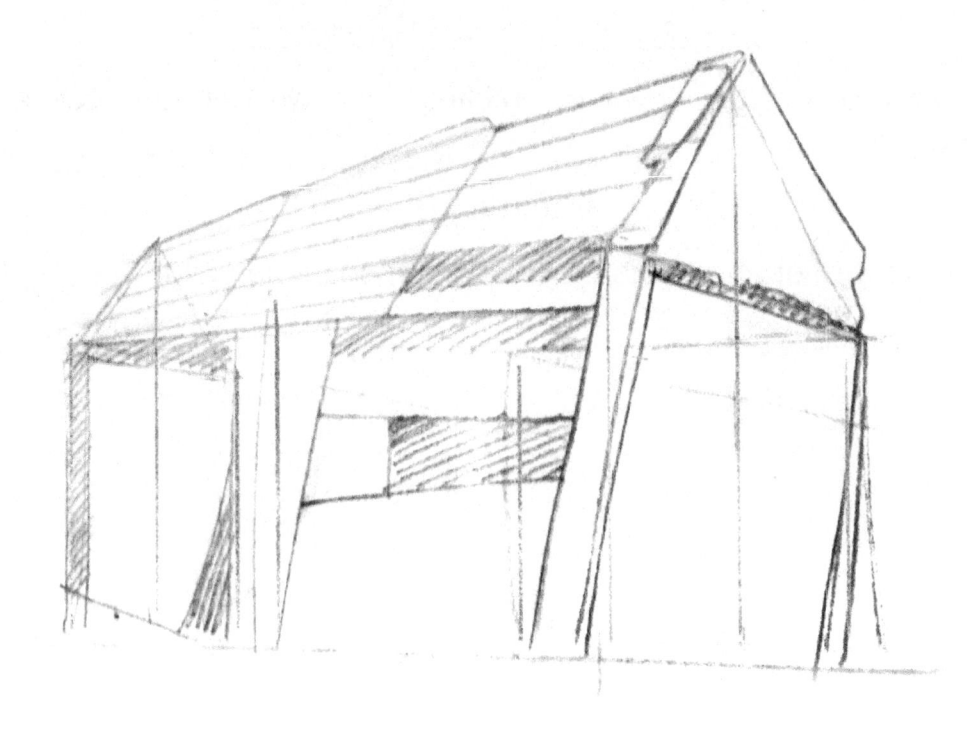

5. Finish the front by taking your pencil and making the thick lines you see in the picture.

6. Draw the bumpy details in the back of the shack.

7. Shade the places shown in the picture above.

8. Add any details you've left out thus far.

9. Add the ladder on the rear of the building.
10. Shade the ladder.
11. Draw the broken ground using jagged lines.
12. Add the rest of the adornments.
13. Add the rest of the shading.

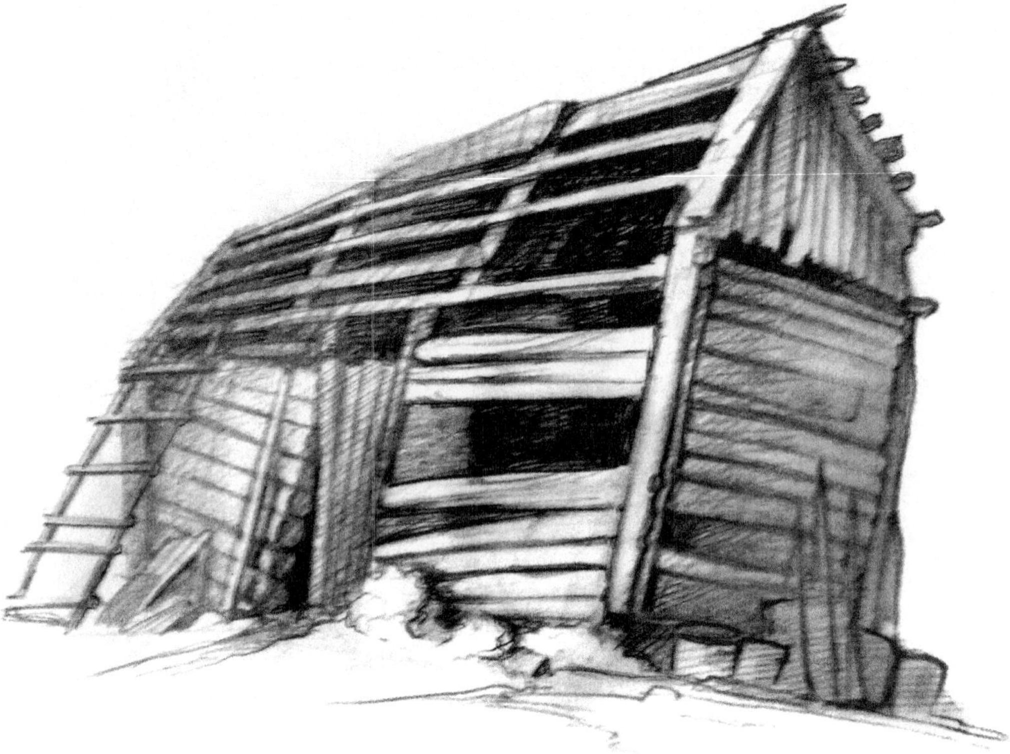

House

1. Use your ruler to draw the beginning of the picture. Start with the support lines and then add the roof.

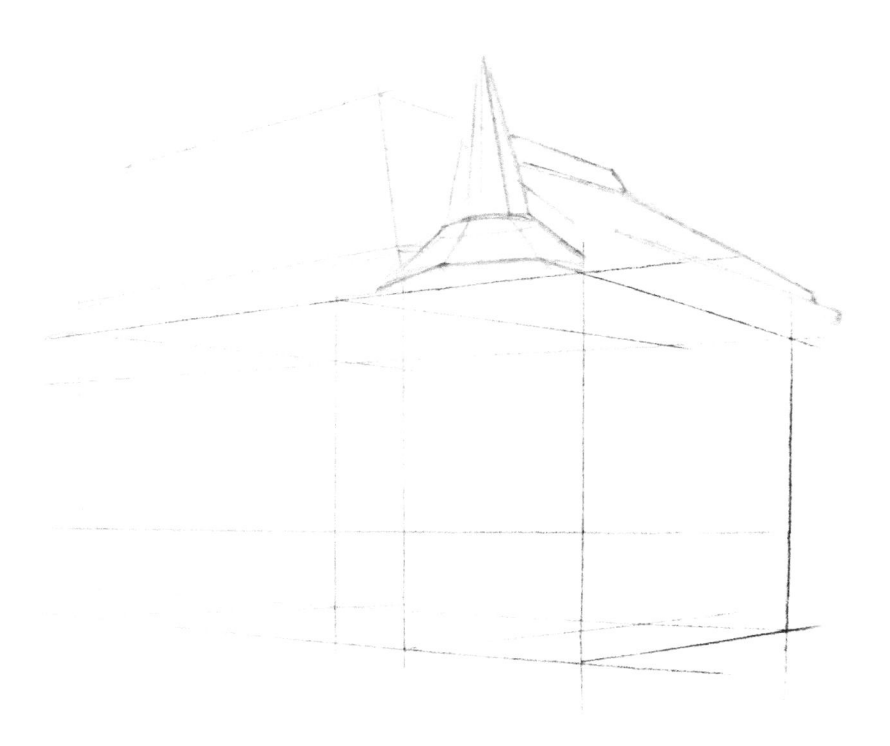

2. Add the windows.
3. Add the sills.
4. Draw the curved arches that support the ceiling.
5. Add the lines on the roof.
6. Add any details you haven't yet.

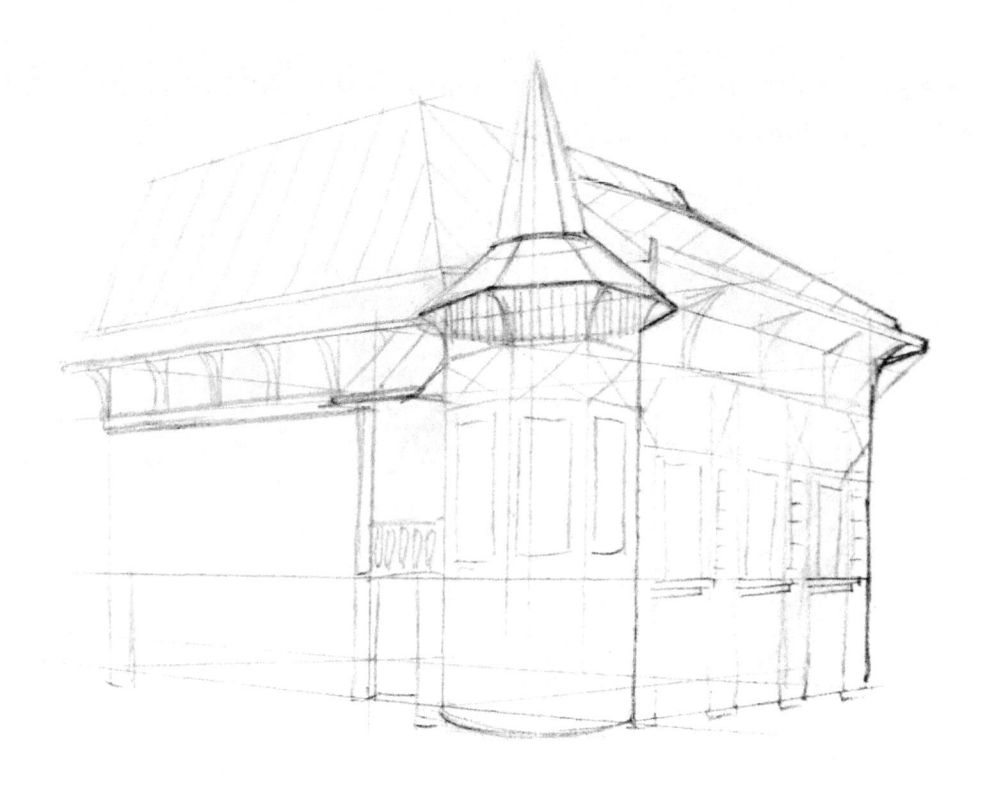

7. Add the "X"s in the picture first.

8. Add the openings on the right side of the picture.

9. Draw in the slants on the front and left side of the picture.

10. On the right side, add the slats and accents for the windows.

11. Add your ledges on the front.

12. By making the lines thicker, you can give depth to any of the accents and windows you need to.

13. Compare and add any details left out.

14. Start shading.

15. Add the lightning rod to the front.

16. Add any decorations you haven't yet.

17. Finish your shading.

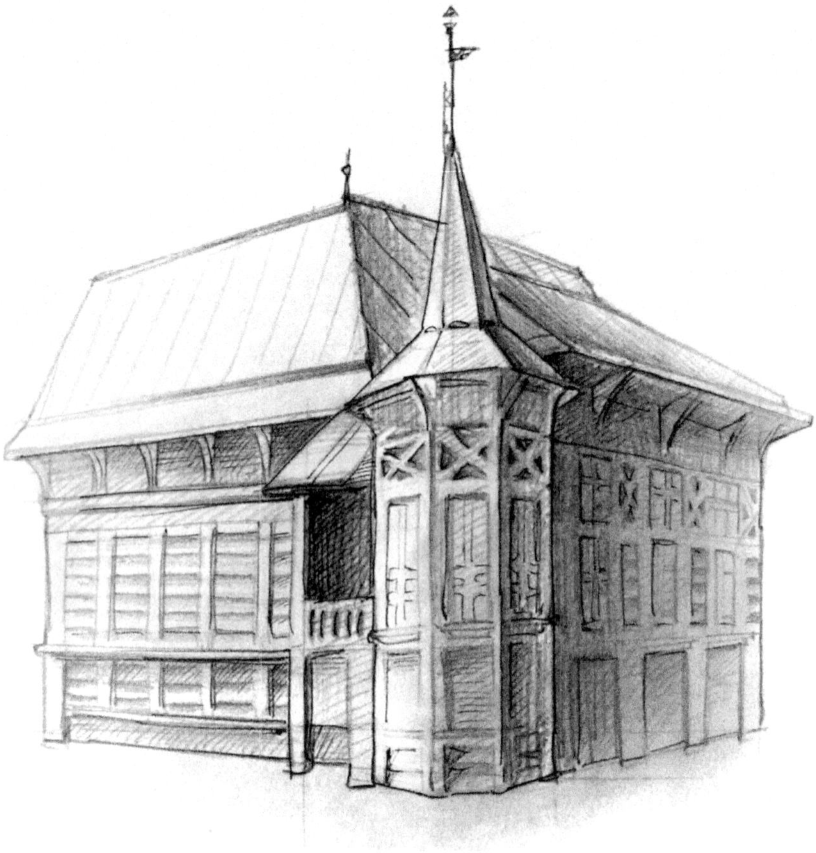

Extra Practice

Chapter 8 - The Human Body

The most difficult is saved for last. The human body is, by far, the most difficult subject to sketch. There are a few things you will need to keep in mind when doing the following lessons:

1. The human body is not symmetrical. This means we are not equally proportioned. One eye is generally more open than then other; one foot is slightly wider, and so forth.

2. The more perfect you try to make the body, less realistic it looks. Draw what you see, not what you would like it to look like.

3. You will need to keep a level head. Patience is key. Don't expect to be able to draw the following lessons perfectly on the first go. You may need to repeat them. That is perfectly fine.

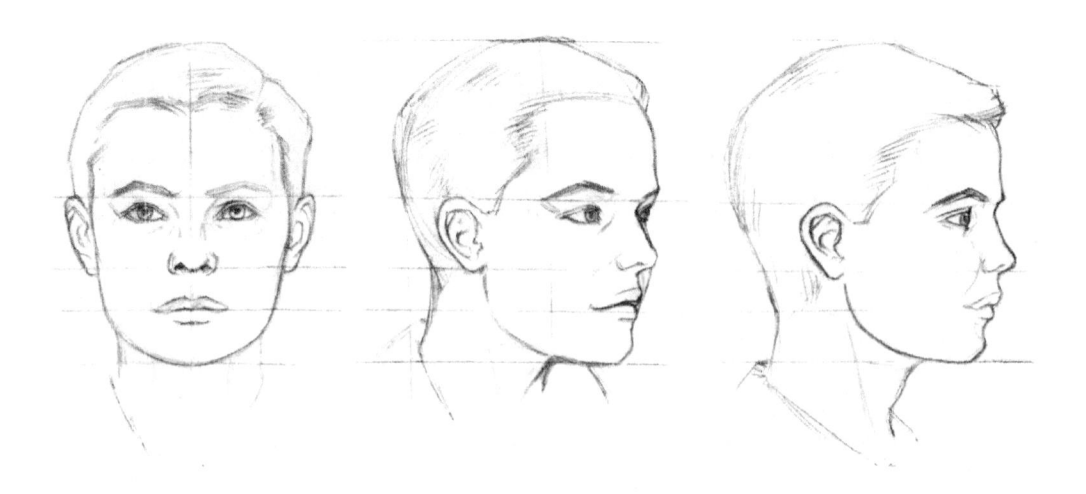

The Female Face

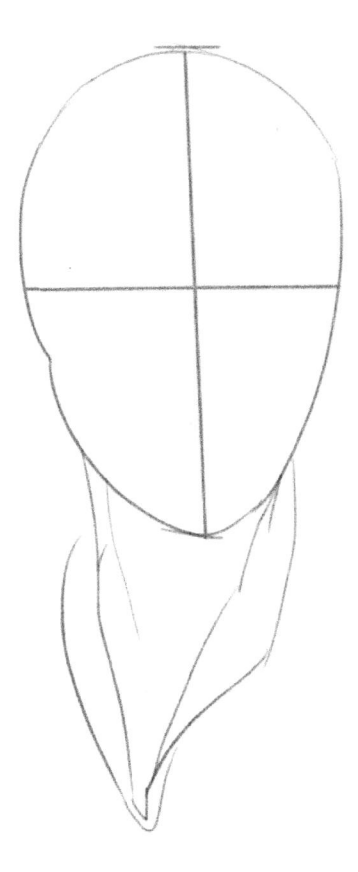

The first thing you will notice is the red cross. This is to help you frame the facial features. We will start from there.

1. Draw the right side of the face.

2. Use the first curve of the left side and stop by curving it in slightly almost all the way down.

3. Finish the curve and connect it to the right side of the face.
4. Draw the curves for the neck.
5. Starting from the neck out, add the collar.
6. Add the guide lines for the face.
7. Make the slight curve on the right side of the face.
8. Draw the curve down the middle of the face.
9. Draw the circles for the eyes.
10. Draw the curves for the bridge of the nose.
11. Draw the curves for the nostrils.

12. Draw the ridge for the nose.
13. Draw the curves for the nostrils.
14. Add the dimples.

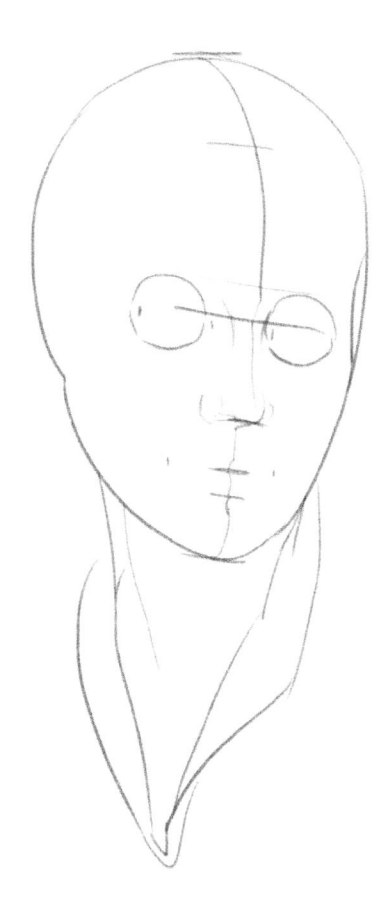

15. Draw the curves for the eyes.
16. Add in the pupils and corneas.
17. Add the beginning of the eyebrows.
18. Add the curves for the lips.

19. Use long, flowing strokes of the pencil for the hair. It doesn't have to look exactly like the picture as long as they look natural.

Before we continue, take note of where the hairline is in relation to the facial features. This is to depict a more natural hairline.

20. Erase all the guide lines.

21. Fill in the brows more.

22. Fill out the nose.

23. Darken the lines a little more.

24. Add the accents under the eyes.

25. Shade in the eyes.

26. On the left side, loosely add the other braid.

27. Using the side of your pencil and your finger, shade your picture as you see to the left.

28. Shade in the hair.
29. Using the eraser and a finger technique, finish the shading.

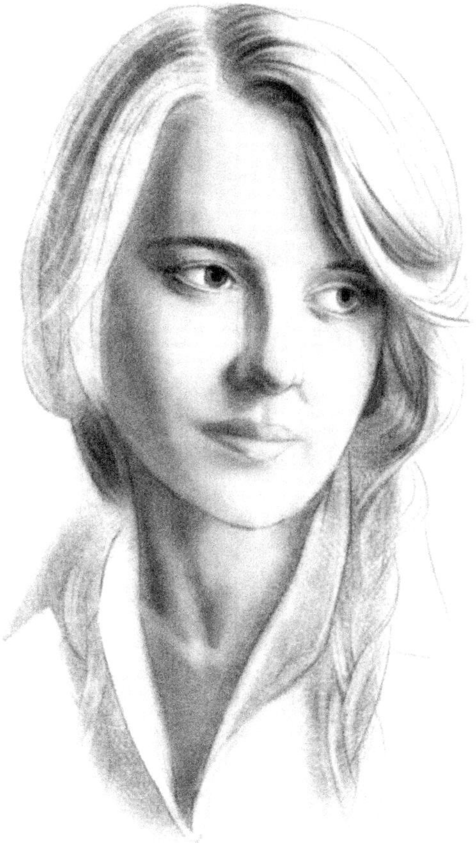

Female Body

1. Draw a vertical line.

2. Equally space the horizontal lines. The different proportions of the body can be measured by the size of the head.

3. Draw a circle to start the head.

4. Draw a curve under the circle for the rest of the head.

5. Where the waist is, draw a sideways head. This is the width of the waist.

6. Draw a curve on each side from the side of the head down to the tip of the hand.

7. Draw a curved "V" for the hand.

8. Draw the curved hand back up to the arm pit. Do this for both sides.

9. Draw one large "U" for each breast.

10. Draw curves for the waist.

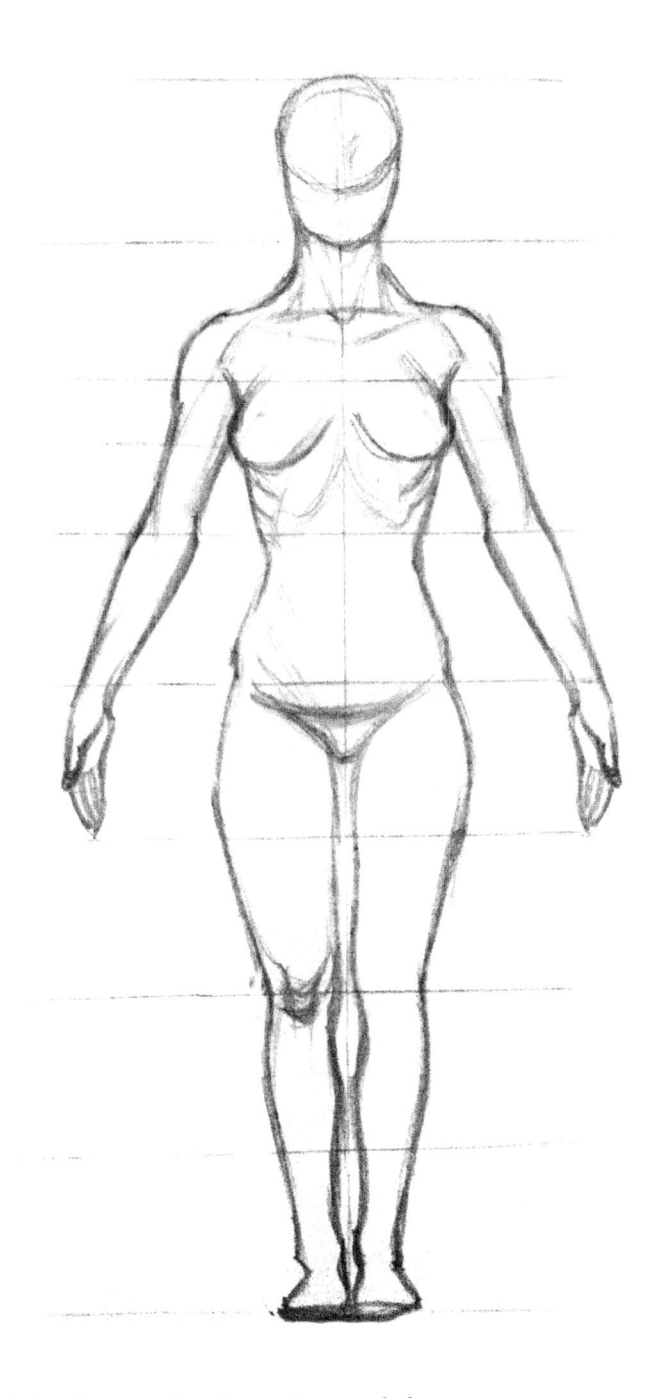

11. Make a slight bump before the pelvis area.

12. Draw the outer curves for the legs.

13. Draw curves for the inner legs.

14. Draw the lines to distinguish the fingers.

15. Draw the curves for the neck to make the muscle tone.

16. Draw the lines and curves for the arms, under the breasts, and the pelvis area.

17. Draw the accents for the knee.

18. Draw a "T" for the features on the face.

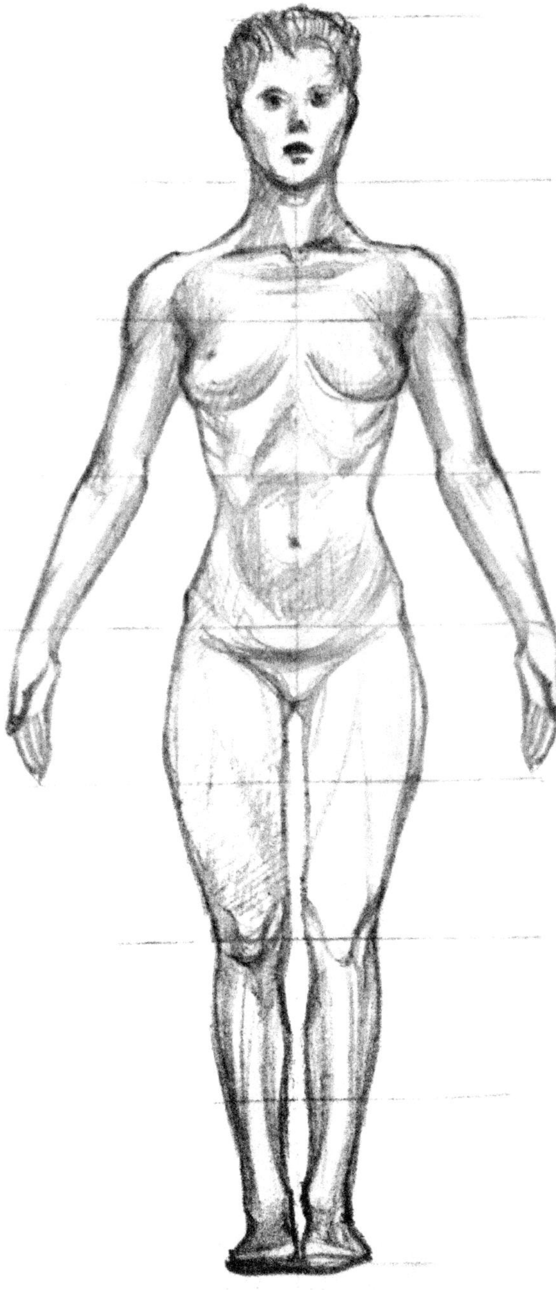

19. Fill in the features.
20. Add the hair by using short, upward strokes.
21. Add the shading you see in the picture.

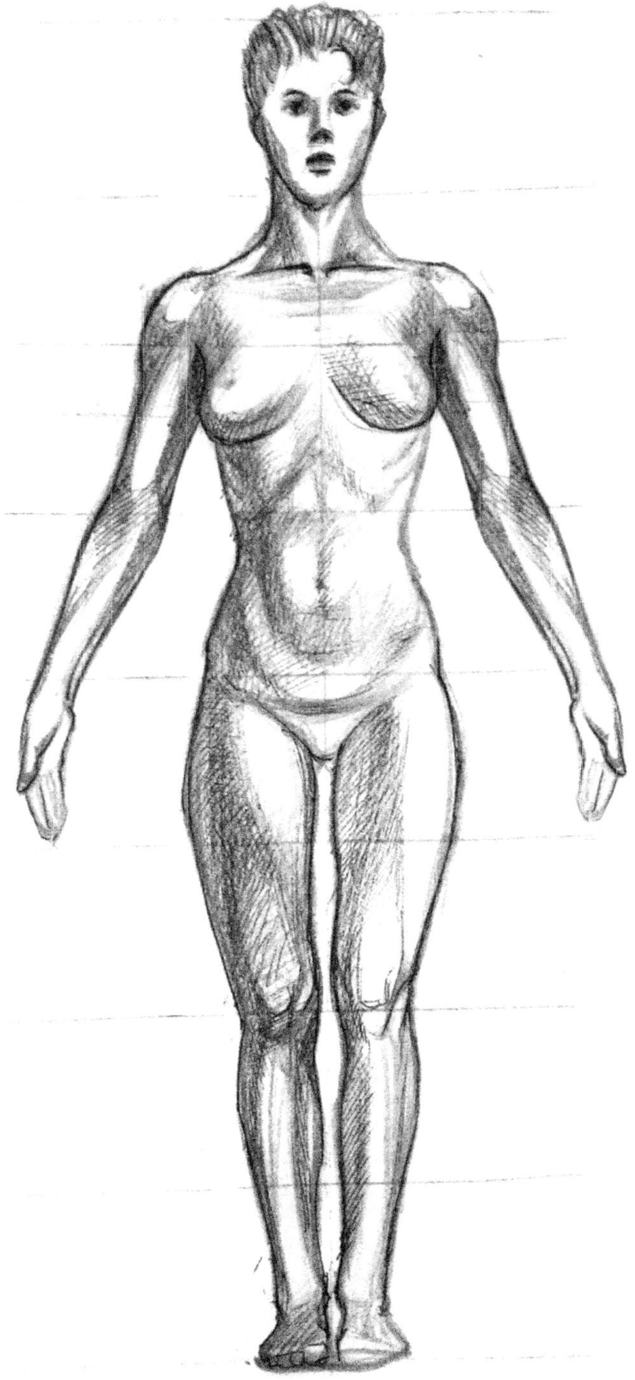

Extra Practice

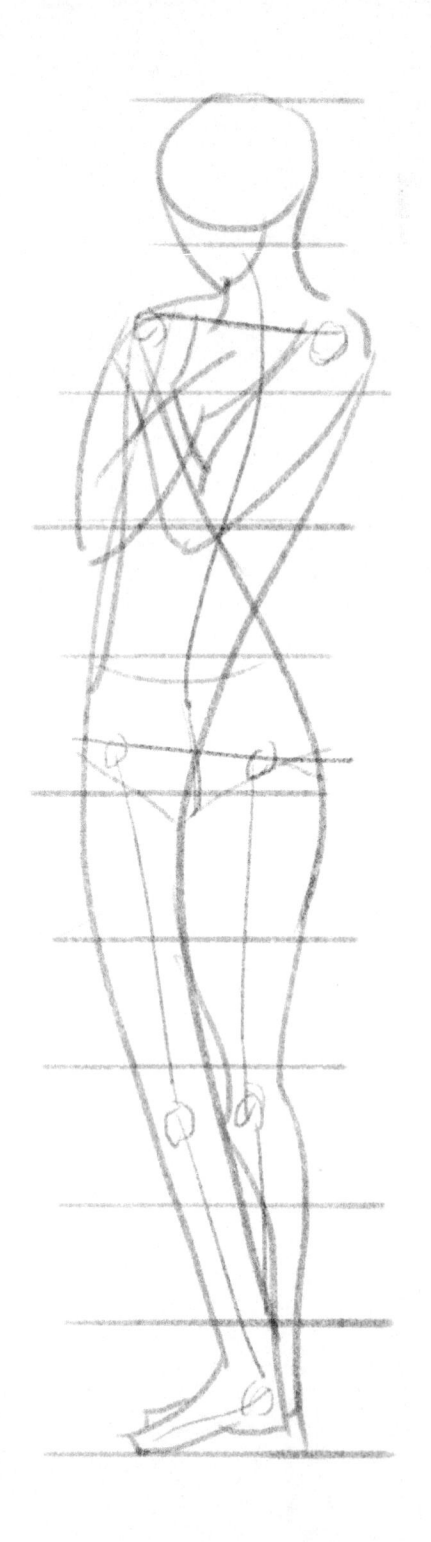

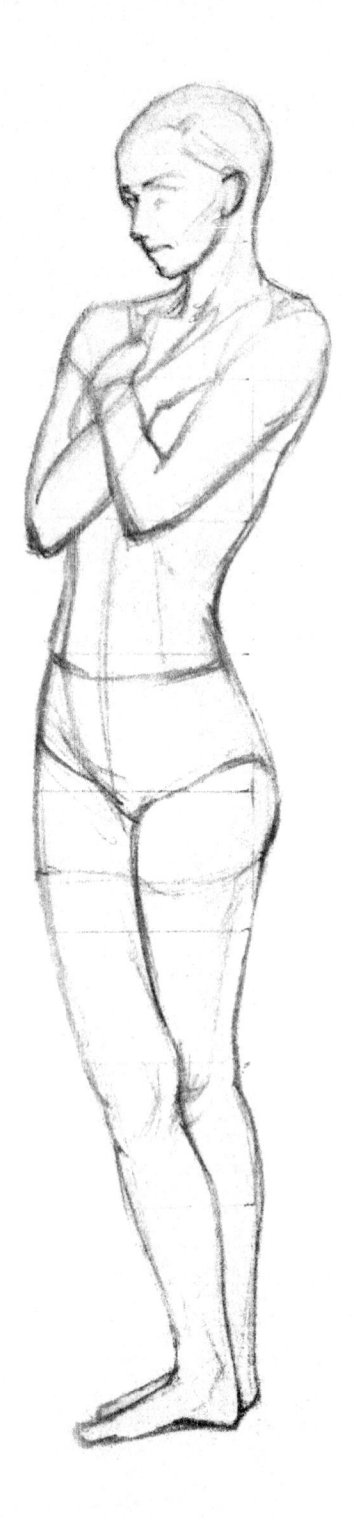

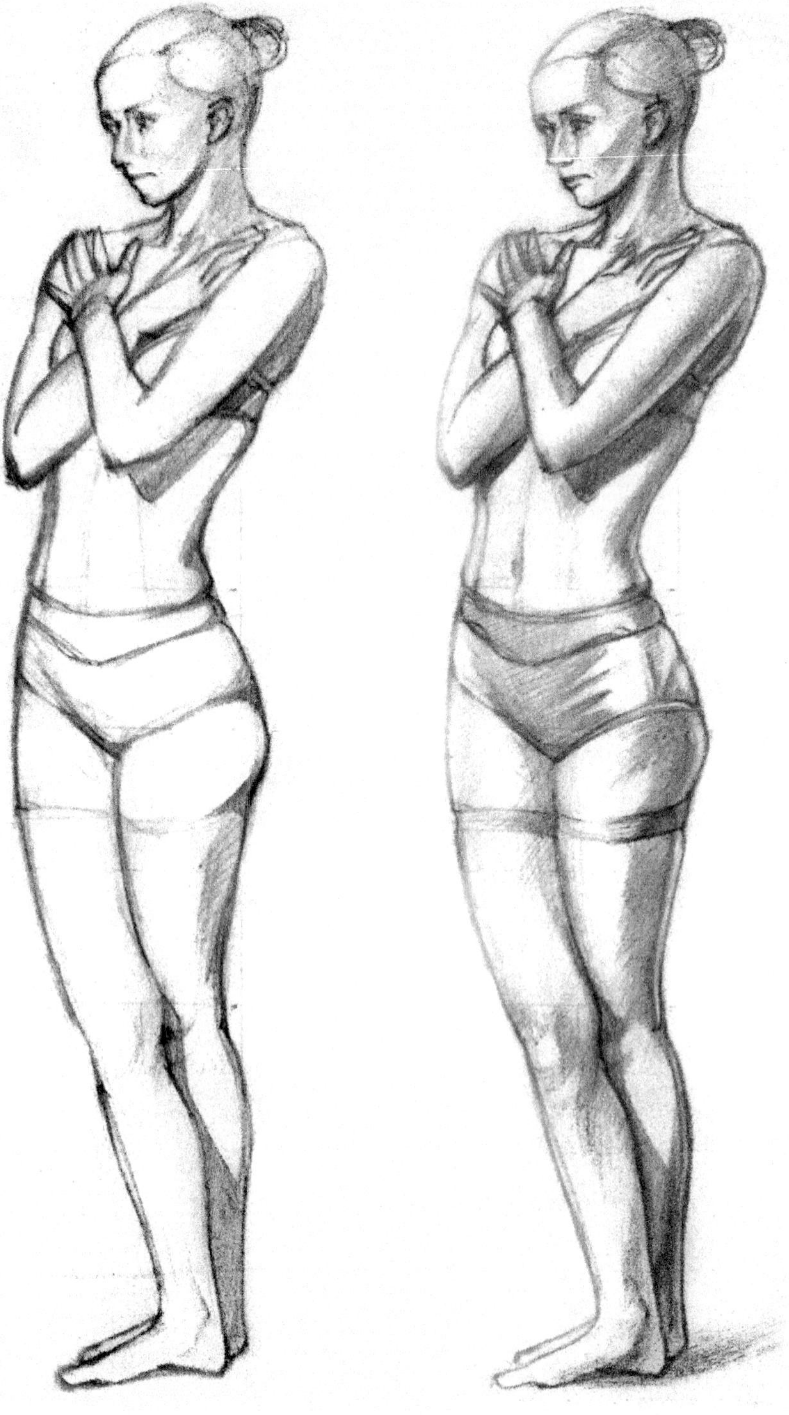

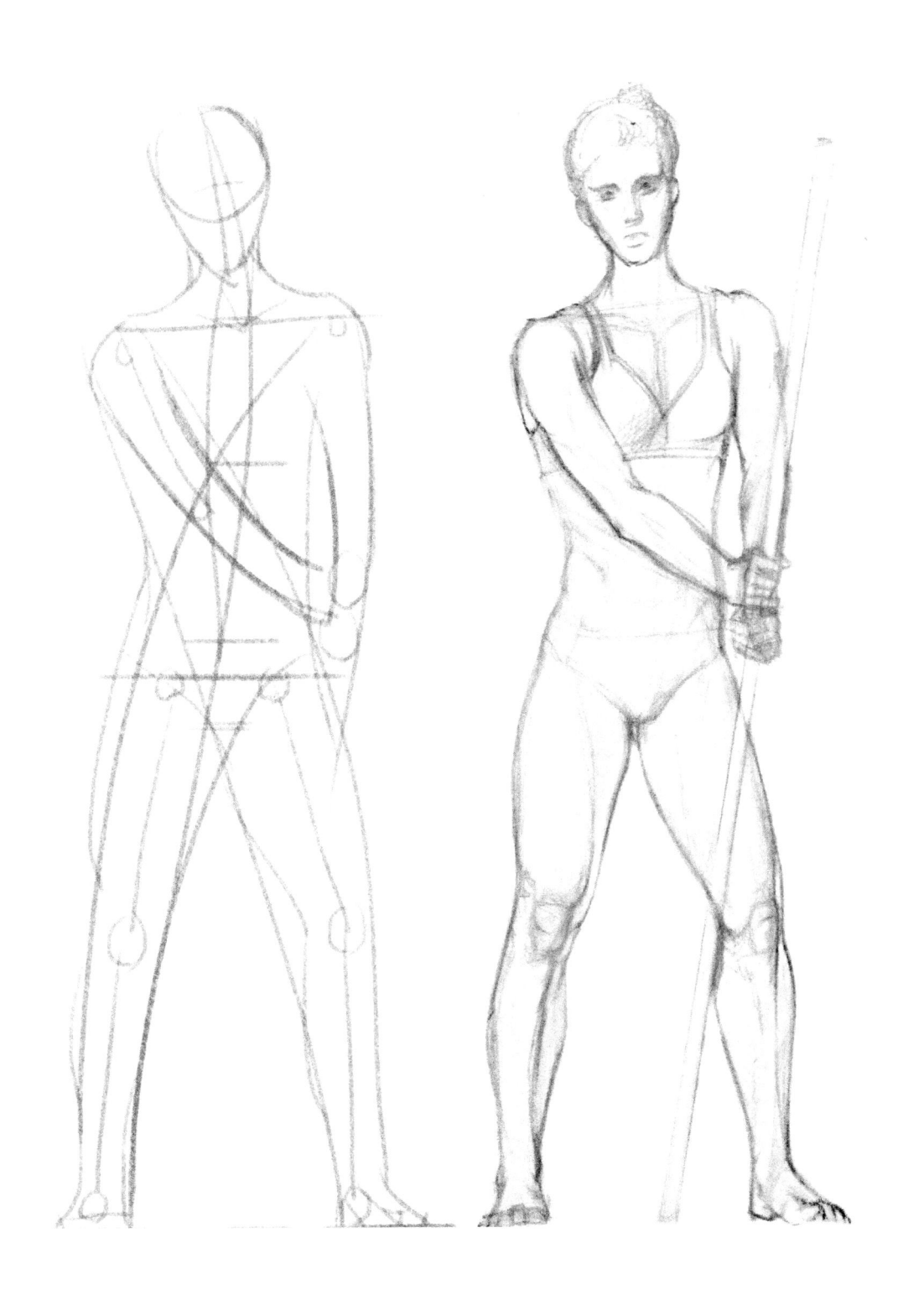

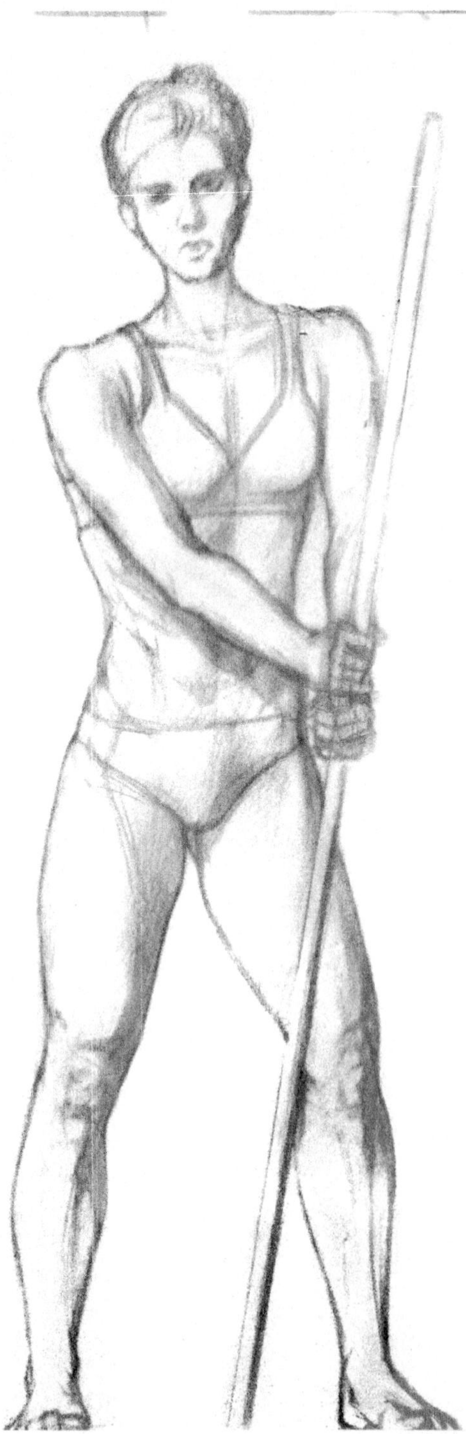

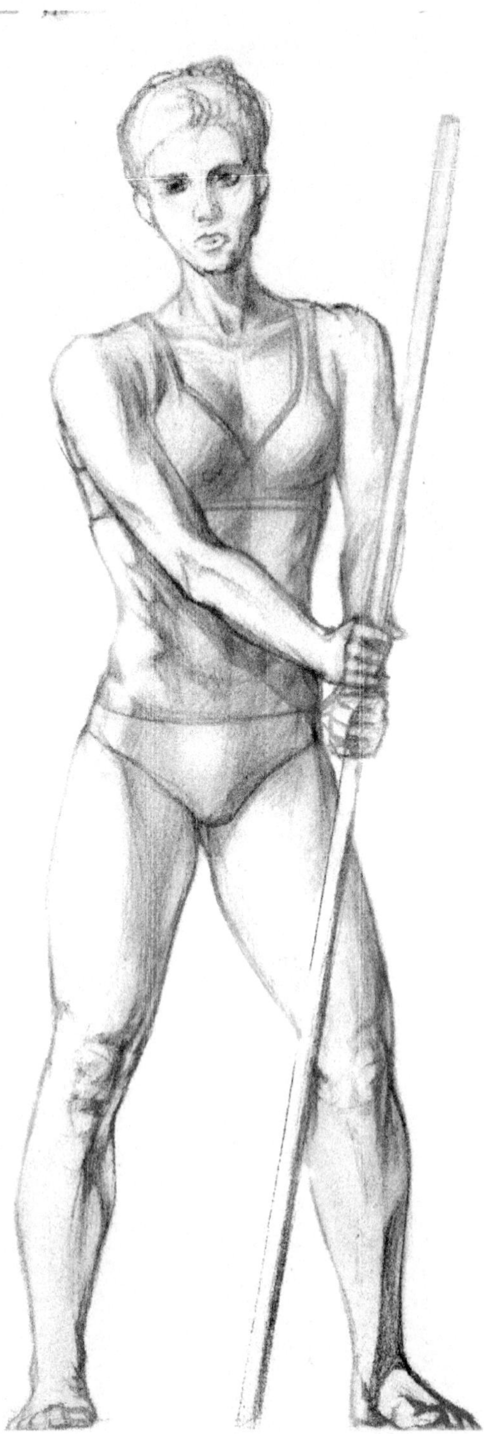

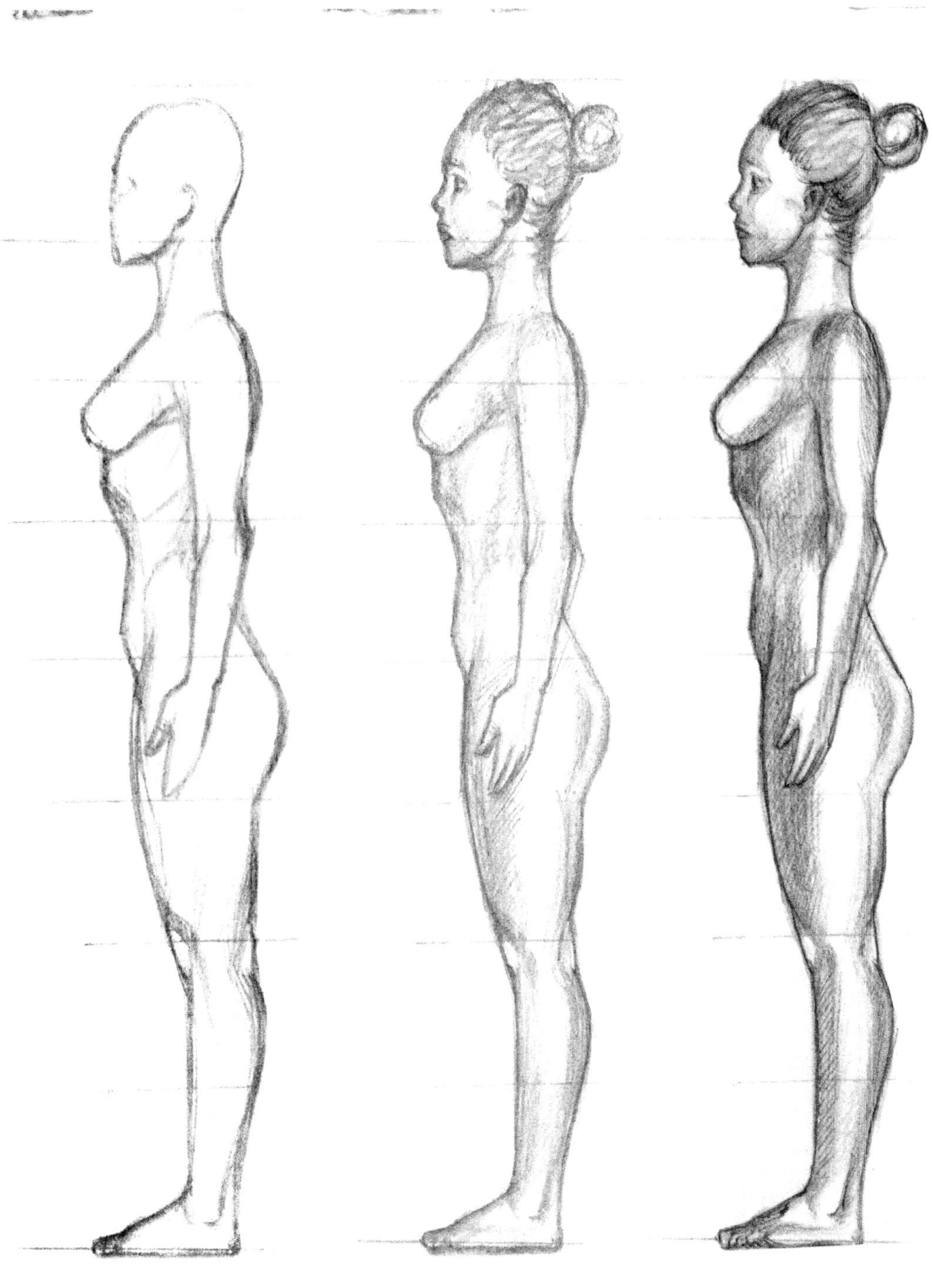

Male Face

1. Using the same technique you did for the female for the beginning of the male.

2. Draw the curves for the ears.

3. Add the small triangles for the details of the ear.

4. Fill in the curves for the head.

5. Draw the curves for the neck.

6. Draw "L"s on each side of the neck for the collar.

7. Draw the lines for the inside of the collar.

8. Finish out the collar.

9. Draw the guide lines you see in the picture. Don't forget the cross lines.

10. Draw the curves for the hair.
11. Draw the circles to help frame the eyes.
12. Draw the curves for the eyes.
13. Draw the curves for the eye brows.
14. Draw in the nose.
15. Draw the wrinkle lines.
16. Draw the curves for the mouth.

17. Darken the hair.
18. Darken the collar.
19. Draw in the lines for the shirt.
20. Fill in the eyebrow.
21. Start the beginning details in the eye.
22. Finish out the lips for the mouth.

23. Erase the guide lines.
24. Start your shading of the picture.

25. Finish your shading.

Male Body

1. Start this like you did the female body. The proportions are the same as the female.

2. Draw the head.

3. Add the bumps for the ears.

4. Add the curves for the neck and shoulders.

5. Use curves for the arms.

6. Add in the hands.

7. Draw the curves back up to the arm pits.

8. Draw the curves for the waist.

9. Add the legs.

10. Add small lines for the toes.

11. All the rest of the missing details.

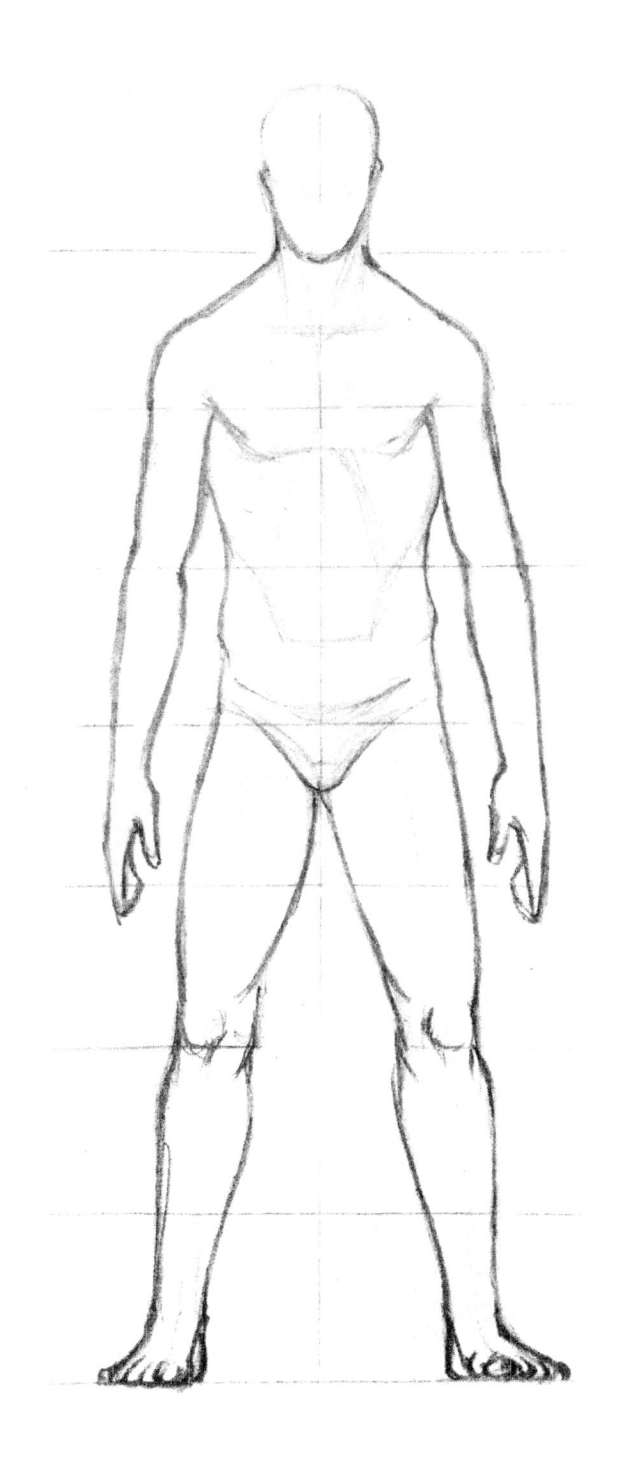

12. Start adding your facial details.
13. Add the muscle lines. Take your time. It's not a race.

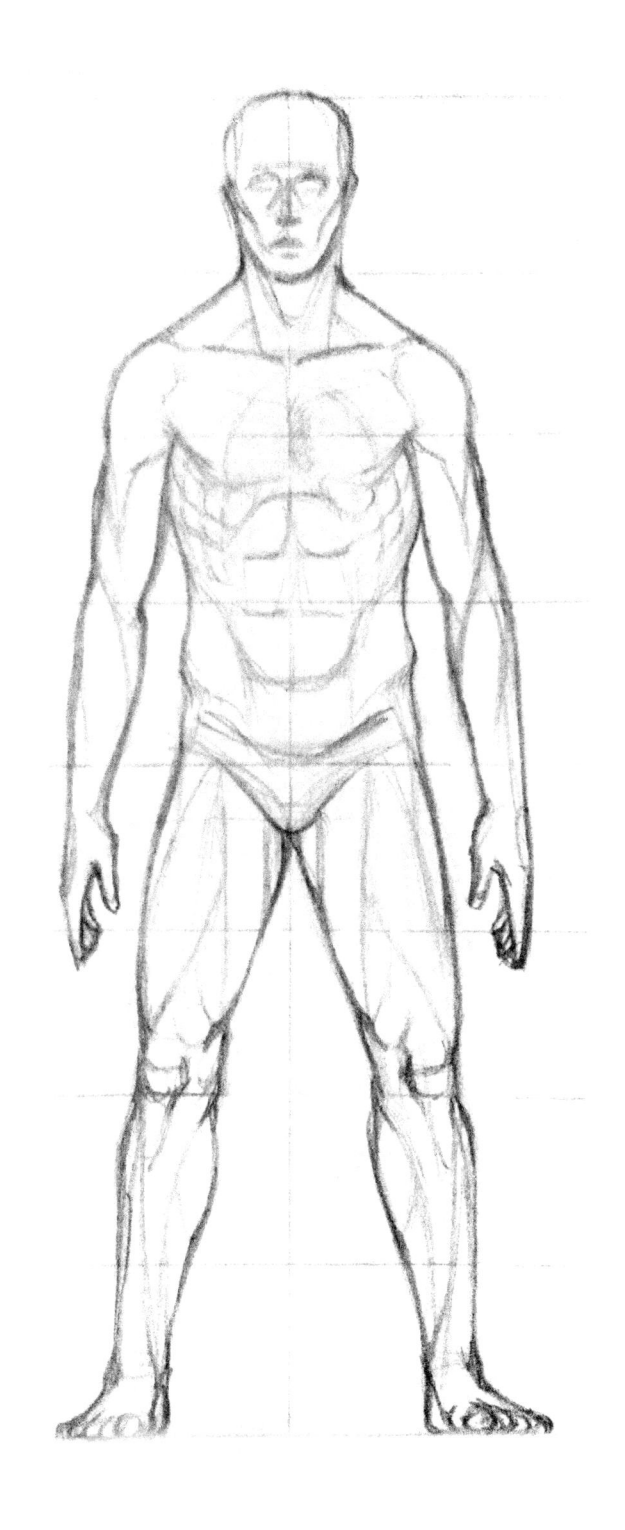

14. Add the shading.

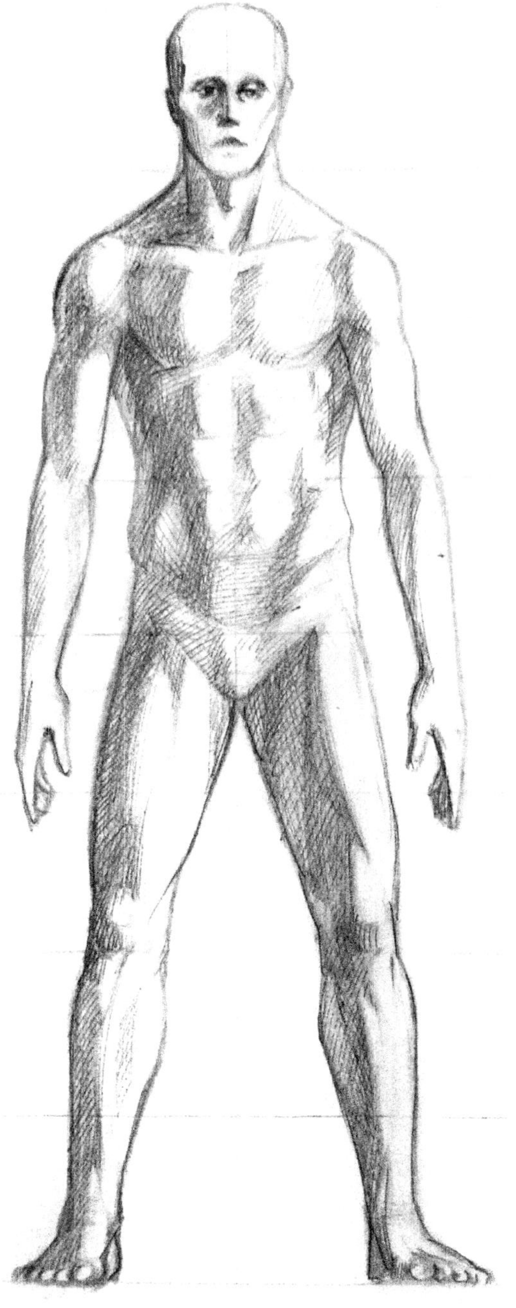

Extra Practice

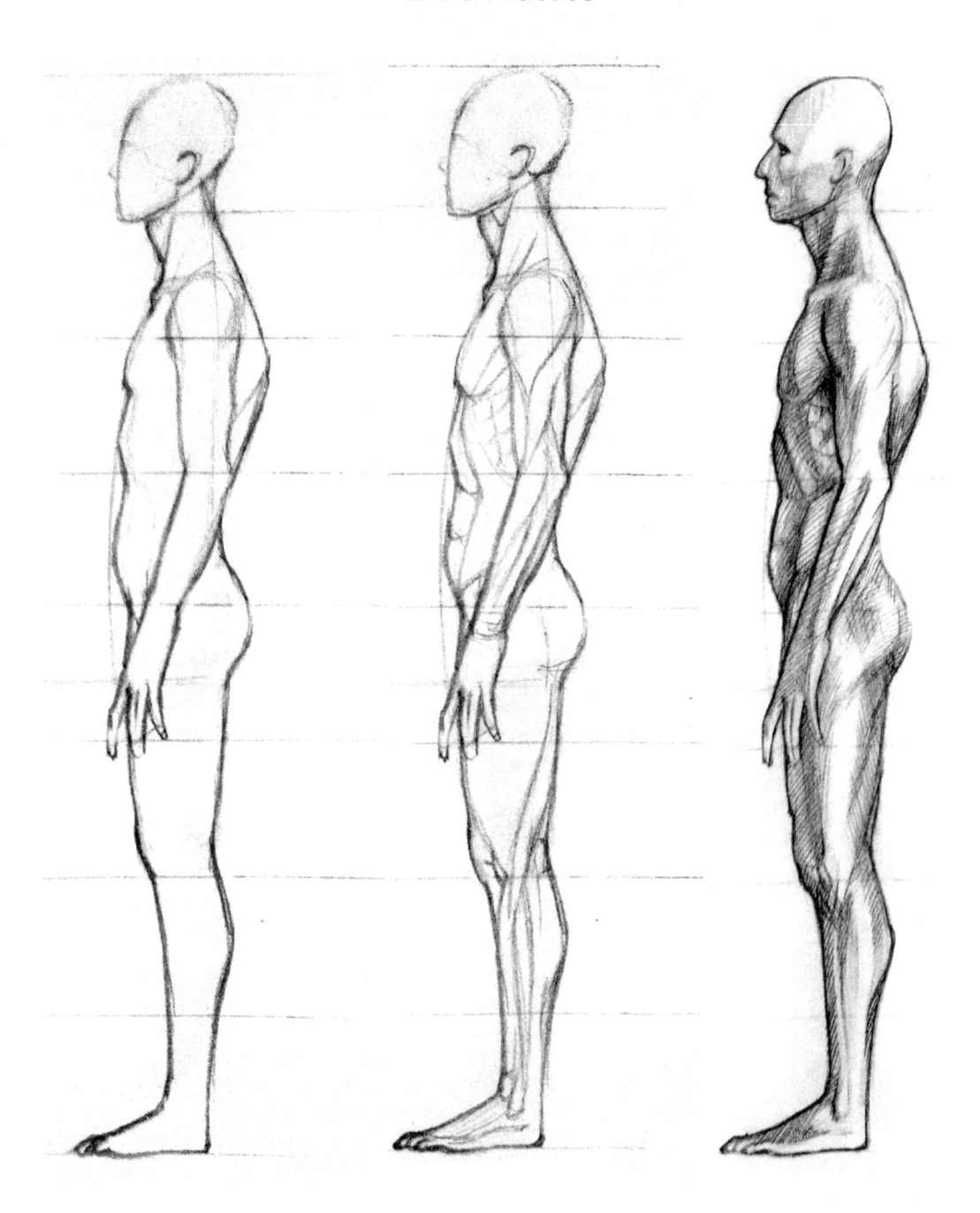

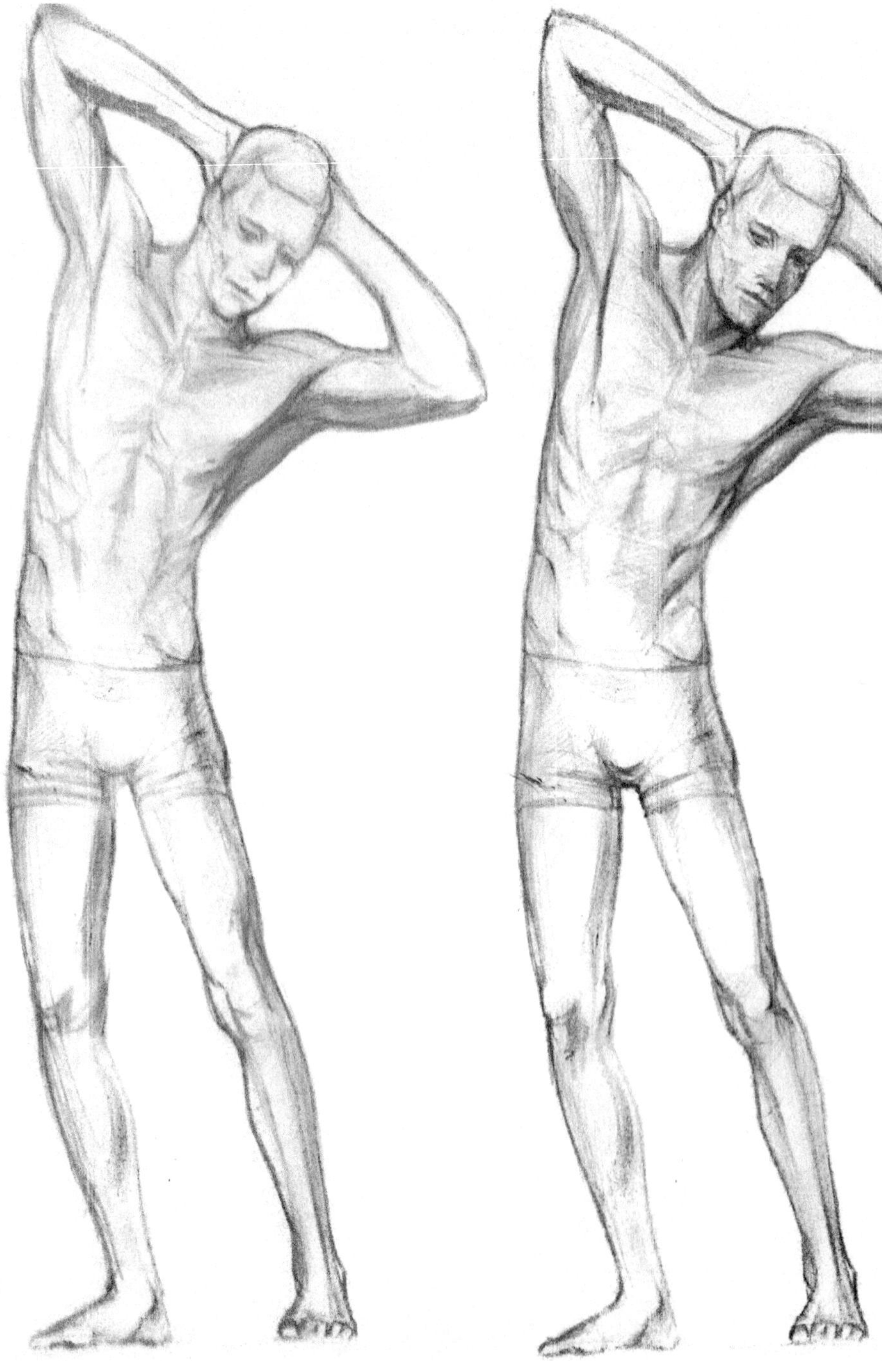

Conclusion

A book's writing is a huge undertaking that calls for commitment, tenacity, and a lot of help. Without the help of so many people and organizations, this work would not have been possible, so I am grateful for their support.

My family and friends have been unwavering in their love and support throughout the writing process, so I want to start by sincerely thanking them. They have consistently inspired me with their support and confidence in me, and I am appreciative of their unwavering dedication to my success.

My mentors and colleagues, who have offered invaluable advice and support along the way, also deserve my sincere gratitude. They generously shared their knowledge and experience with me, and I am appreciative of how their comments, criticisms, and insights helped to shape this work.

I would like to thank the institutions and groups for their support, funding, and resources for my study and writing. I am grateful for the opportunities they have given me to pursue this project with rigor and dedication because of their support, which has allowed me to conduct thorough research and write a high-quality manuscript.

I also want to express my gratitude to the production team, editors, and designers who put in countless hours to make this book a reality. I am appreciative of their hard work and commitment to this project because their meticulous attention to detail, professionalism, and commitment to excellence have greatly influenced the final product.

I want to express my gratitude to the many people who have made both significant and insignificant contributions to this work. I am incredibly appreciative of all of your contributions, from the experts who so kindly shared their knowledge and experience with me to the reviewers who thoughtfully commented on the manuscript to the readers who engaged with the content and offered perceptive comments and questions.

Finally, I'd like to thank the larger group of academics and thinkers who provided this work with inspiration and guidance. Their arguments, discussions, and ideas have enriched my knowledge of the world and influenced how I have approached this project. I am thankful for the chance to participate in this ongoing discussion.

I want to thank everyone who has helped with this work from the bottom of my heart. Your assistance, direction, and knowledge have been crucial to the success of this project, and I am honored to have had the opportunity to collaborate with such outstanding people and organizations.

Brianh .D Carpenterl

Printed in Great Britain
by Amazon